WRITERS AND THEIR WORK

ISOBEL ARMSTRONG
General Editor

BRYAN LOUGHREY
Advisory Editor

Aphra Behn

APHRA BEHN
from an engraving by FITTLER *of 1822 after a portrait attributed to* MARY BEALE
National Portrait Gallery, London

WWW

Aphra
Behn

S. J. Wiseman

Northcote House

in association with
The British Council

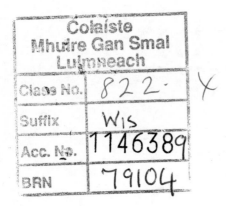
© Copyright 1996 by S. J. Wiseman

First published in 1996 by Northcote House Publishers Ltd, Plymbridge House,
Estover Road, Plymouth PL6 7PZ, United Kingdom.
Tel: (01752) 735251. Fax: (01752) 695699.

British Library Cataloguing-in-Publication Data
A catalogue record for this book is available from the British Library

ISBN 0 7463 0709 8

Typeset by PDQ Typesetting, Newcastle-Under-Lyme
Printed and bound in the United Kingdom by BPC Wheatons Ltd, Exeter

Contents

Acknowledgements

Thanks are due to Professor Isobel Armstrong for commissioning this text and for her kindness and patience during revisions. Thanks, too, to Christina Zaba for grappling with the text, for meticulous editing, and for steering the text towards clarity. Thanks also to Brian Hulme at Northcote House. Tim Armstrong, Kate Chedgzoy, Helen Hackett, Tom Healy, Bryan Loughrey, and Jane Milling all read parts of the manuscript and I am grateful for their comments. For conversations, thanks to Ros Ballaster, Claire Buck, Susan Bruce, Cathy Cundy, Rod Edmond, Lyn Innes, Kate Lilley, Jan Montefiore, Susan J. Owen, Cath Sharrock, the research group, and students on Gender and Identity 1992–3, 1993–4 at the University of Kent. Dr Boika Sokolova and Professor Alexander Shurnabov kindly invited me to give a paper at Sofia, and I am grateful for the response and criticism there. Thanks, too, to the staff of the British Library and the libraries of Sheffield and Warwick Universities. Finally, thanks to Pinky and Perky.

Biographical Outline

*c.*1640	Birth of Aphra Johnson in Kent. May be Behn.
1642	English Civil War begins.
1648	English Civil War ends.
1649	Charles I beheaded in Whitehall. England becomes a republic.
1653	Protectorate of Oliver Cromwell.
1658	Cromwell dies.
1659	Breakdown of rival governments. John Milton publishes *The Readie and Easie Way to a Free Commonwealth*.
1660	Charles Stuart returns to England with his brother, James, Duke of York, who is a Roman Catholic. Coronation of Charles II. Two theatre companies granted patents by Charles II and run by Sir William Davenant and Sir Thomas Killigrew. Killigrew's contract with players includes an agreement to use actresses.
1663	Behn may have visited Surinam.
1664–5	Conjectural date used by some biographers for Behn's assumed marriage and consequent change of name from conjectural maiden name of Johnson.
1666–7	Behn in Antwerp working as government agent.
1669	Frances Boothby's play, *Marcelia*, performed.
1670	Behn's *The Forced Marriage* performed.
1671	William Wycherley's first play, *Love in a Wood*, performed.
1672	*Covent Garden Drolery, or a Collection Of all the Choice Songs, Poems, Prologues, and Epilogues* possibly edited by Behn.
1675	William Wycherley's *The Country Wife* staged.
1676	*Abdelazar* performed by Duke's company, Behn's only tragedy. Etherege's *Man of Mode* and Wycherley's *The*

Plain Dealer produced. *The Town Fop, or Sir Timothy Tawdry* staged.

1677   *The Rover I* performed at Dorset Garden by the Duke's company. Elizabeth Barry plays Hellena (in *The Rover II* she played the prostitute).

1678   Scandal of a 'Popish Plot' against the Government reported to Charles II. *Sir Patient Fancy* probably staged.

1679   Behn's *The Feign'd Curtezans* staged. 'To Madam Behn' by 'Ephelia', published in *Female Poems on Several Occasions.*

1680   John Wilmot Earl of Rochester dead. A pirated edition of his poems printed, *Poems upon Several Occasions By the Right Honourable Earl of R——*, including Behn's 'The Disappointment' and other poems by her.

1681   Thomas Shadwell's *The Lancashire Witches* produced as power of radicals faded. *The Roundheads* staged.

1682   Execution of Protestants and republicans. Lady Henrietta Berkeley runs away with her brother-in-law Ford, Lord Grey of Werke. John Dryden's play, *The Duke of Guise*, produced. *The City Heiress* staged by Duke's Company. Elizabeth Barry as Lady Galliard. Trouble over Behn's epilogue to *Romulus and Herselia* attacking Monmouth. Poems published by Nathaniel Thompson.

1683   Extant letter from Behn to publisher Jacob Tonson states that she is 'just on the point of breaking', her poverty exacerbated by the loss of income from the theatre.

1684   Behn's *Love Letters between a Nobleman and his Sister* (I) and her collection *Poems Upon Several Occasions: With a Voyage to the Island of Love* published.

1685   Death of Charles II. James II succeeds. Fulsome congratulatory poem by Behn. Monmouth's Rebellion defeated at Sedgemoor in West Country. *Miscellany, Being a collection of Poems By several Hands* includes poems by Behn and others. Dryden's *Albion and Albanius* produced.

1686   Severe reprisals against 1,300 plotters. Behn's *The Lucky Chance* staged by the combined company at Drury Lane.

1687   Behn's *Love Letters* published. *Aesop's Fables with his Life in English, French and Latin* illustrated by Francis Barlow. Reprint of 1666 edition, with the English versions done by Behn.

1688   James II forced to fly to France. Waits for French wind in the same chamber from which his father had been executed. William and Mary invited to rule. *The Fair Jilt* (with Behn's name on the title-page) and *Oroonoko* published. *Lycidus, or the Lover in Fashion ... Together with a Miscellany of New Poems* edited by Behn. Includes her previously unpublished poems, and *Lycidus*, a continuation of the translation earlier published as *Voyage to the Isle of Love*.

1689   Anglican bishop and historian, Gilbert Burnet, invites Behn to support the new regime. She replies with 'A Pindaric Poem to The Reverend Doctor Burnet'. *The Second and Third Parts of the Works of Mr. Abraham Cowley ... containing his Six Books of Plant* published, translations by Behn. She dies and is buried in Westminster Abbey. Her *The Widow Ranter*, recapitulating events of 1670s in Virginia, is staged.

1695   Ariadne's *She Ventures and He Wins* staged at the New Theatre, Lincoln's Inn. Preface honours Behn. Catherine Trotter's play, based on Behn's story, *Agnes de Castro*, staged.

1696   *Novels and Histories* published by Charles Gildon with memoir by 'One of the Fair Sex'. *The Unfortunate Bride* published. *The Younger Brother* staged.

Abbreviations

Where available the edition of the *Works of Aphra Behn*, vols i-iv by Janet Todd (London 1992–5) has been used. All other references are to the edition of the *Works of Aphra Behn*, vols i-vi by Montague Summers (London, 1915). Full publication details are given in the Select Bibliography. The following abbreviations have been used in citing works: volume numbers are set in Roman numerals; poetry references have a volume number, page number, and line numbers; drama references have a volume number, act and scene numbers in Roman numerals, and page numbers; prose references have a volume number followed by a page number. Thus:

Poetry   Todd, ii. 123. 4–8.
Drama   Summers, iii. v. iv. 5.
Prose   Todd, iv. 17.

1

Introduction

This book introduces the reader to a range of texts written by Aphra Behn. Behn wrote a vast quantity of material: Montague Summers's edition remains incomplete at six large volumes. Her work, as opposed to her life, is only now coming fully to the attention of critics. Behn has long been the focus of historical and feminist study – she is, for example, an important figure in Virginia Woolf's *A Room of One's Own* – and there have been several biographies and assessments of her fascinating life. These biographies have dealt with literary texts, but this study is a non-biographical book devoted to her writings. For that reason, and because discussion has so often concentrated on only one or two of her texts, I have chosen to write short essays on most of the genres she wrote in, attempting to introduce both Behn's best-known texts and a range of her less-known writings.

There are sections on the two texts which are usually taken as representative of Behn's writing, the play *The Rover* and the fictional piece *Oroonoko, or the Royal Slave*. But in each case these texts are within sections dealing with a range of Behn's output in drama and prose. A reader can compare *The Rover* with Behn's other comedies, or set the concerns of *Oroonoko* alongside the other fiction she wrote. By organizing the volume by genre – poetry first, then plays, and finally prose – it has been possible to follow roughly the chronology of Behn's writing. Behn wrote and published poetry throughout her life, but the period of her greatest theatrical output coincided with the dominance of the stage in English cultural life from the late 1670s to the mid-1680s. Then, when the theatre failed as a source of income for writers, she turned to the emerging market for prose narratives. The longer fictions such as *Love Letters between a Nobleman and his Sister* and *Oroonoko* belong to the last years of her life, the later 1680s.

Aphra Behn's prodigious literary output was bound to the commercial genres of her time, to the institutions of publishing performance, and reading dominant in Restoration London. She wrote *marketable* texts. For this reason, and because she wrote so much, her *œuvre* does not fit neatly into the idea of an author as someone who develops certain central ideas throughout her life. Behn's texts are often linked to quite specific circumstances of the market and of politics. This is true of her satirical political poems, her plays, and *Love Letters between a Nobleman and his Sister*, which reworks a contemporary sexual and political scandal. Anyone searching for the 'major issues' which dominate Behn's work must also take account of the way momentary contingencies affected the writing of these texts, and of the narrative shapes provided by different genres. While Restoration comedy, for example, allowed the possibility of unpunished sexual transgression, this was a more problematic issue in narrative prose, and was dealt with rather differently. The reader may wish, therefore, to compare the legal separation in *Sir Patient Fancy* with the drastic solutions of Miranda in the short fictional piece *The Fair Jilt*.

Despite such diversities of time and genre, there are certain issues to which her texts return again and again, though critics would certainly differ in deciding what these are. In choosing issues to concentrate on I have heeded Catherine Gallagher's warning that, 'when space is limited, the works of the protean and inconsistent writer will always be trimmed to fit someone's idea of the real Aphra Behn'.[1] The study which follows discusses selected issues in relation to all the different genres Behn worked in. But I have not tried to claim that in writing about these I have found 'the real Aphra Behn'.

The issues that this book concentrates on are: desire (especially female desire), politics, and formal questions of narration. In poetry, comedy, and prose Behn's writing returns to the question of female desire. The term 'desire' implies not only sexual desire – though certainly her texts treat this again and again – but also the desire for social and economic security. Her texts explore what it means to want something, or need something, and they juxtapose political and sexual desires with economic needs.

Behn's writing also repeatedly returns to political questions. It both puts into circulation political positions and, at times, offers critiques of sexual, national, and colonial politics. While this book deals with politics in most detail in relation to her plays at the time of the Exclusion Crisis, political issues permeate her poetry and fiction too. Indeed, it is impossible to make sense of her work without some understanding of the political issues of her time (the reader may wish to refer to the biographical timeline, and the question of politics and writing is discussed below). Behn saw politics as an integral part of her writing. She was a 'Tory' writer – an apologist for Charles II and, after his death in 1685, for his brother, the Roman Catholic King James II. But as well as the overt message of many of her texts – that the Stuarts are good and their attackers bad – her writing enters into a complex relationship with the politics she opposes.

Paradoxically, a *frisson* of fascination with republicanism and with the Whig policies and activities which Behn officially opposed animates much of her work, including the long fiction *Love Letters between a Nobleman and his Sister*, the political poetry, and the polemical comedies such as *Sir Patient Fancy*, *The City Heiress*, and *The Lucky Chance*. This fascination – a highly charged excitement about analysis of the forbidden – brings the reader into contact with forbidden figures and politics, encouraging him or her, for example, to feel sympathy for Charles II's illegitimate son, the Duke of Monmouth. And in *Love Letters* the text opens with an invitation to empathize with the thoughts and feelings of the protagonists who are also, simultaneously, the objects of the text's satire. It is this combination of intimacy and satire which characterizes Behn's pervasive use of the political in her texts, inviting the reader to be fascinated by political transgression, even to empathize with it and understand it. But at the same time she repudiates the transgression and its perpetrators; and the section in Chapter 4 on *Oroonoko* juxtaposes questions of authority and transgression with the way Behn's texts invite us to be fascinated by cultural difference, by cultural 'others'.

A linking thread in Behn's texts, displayed through the differing strategies of poetry, prose, and drama, but always present, is the manipulation of the reader by the way the story is told. In addition, as in *Love Letters*, the texts investigate the relationship between eloquence and sincerity. Indeed, the third aspect of Behn's texts which this study discusses is the power of storytelling or narration. Chapter 2 analyses the way in which the power to tell a story gives the teller some control over events; Chapter 3 examines the way in which the crisis of the 1670s and 1680s is posed in Behn's plays as a triumph of gallants and ladies, a triumph proposed as 'winner's history'. And Chapter 4 considers the relationship between power and eloquence, culminating in a longer section on the re-location of all Behn's central concerns in Surinam. In a sense, the whole issue of the power of storytelling is thrown into question by *Oroonoko* because in this, the last text discussed in the book, it is never clear who can speak, or on what authority. This crisis in eloquence signals the text's problematic relationship to some of the contradictory logics of European expansion.

WHO WAS APHRA BEHN?

Who was this woman who, at a period when very few women wrote at all, produced such a vast quantity of writing? One answer has to be that, although more biographical information is coming to light, we know relatively little about her apart from her career in writing and that she worked briefly as a spy.[2]

What *do* we know about the Behn who walked in the world? She may have been born Aphra Johnson in Kent in 1640, where she may have had some connection to the aristocratic Culpeppers. She may have gone to Surinam in the later 1650s and 1660s. This is claimed as fact by many biographers; but the best one can say is that the circumstantial detail offered by *Oroonoko* is strong, and she asserts the connection again in the preface to *The Young King*. In 1666–7 we know she was calling herself Astrea, working as a spy in an attempt to extract information from William Scot, the son of the regicide Thomas Scot. We know from papers in the Public Record Office that while spying she ran up debts of £150, which none of the government officials (not Halsall nor Arlington nor Killigrew, the theatre manager) would pay. She wrote that she was about to be taken to prison. She may have married a Mr Behn. And after this point, despite speculation about a relationship with the lawyer John Hoyle and her Roman Catholicism, we have a lot of information not about her, but about her literary output. We know that she had an active career in literary spheres which were then usually the province of men alone. She edited volumes of poetry, produced plays whose dedications and epilogues hint at her literary and political connections, wrote panegyric poetry for James II and satires on his enemies. She knew the most eminent poets and playwrights of her time; she worked alongside Dryden. And when she wrote for the theatre, from the 1670s to the mid-1680s, she knew the playwrights (including Otway) and the actors (including Nell Gwyn). As opportunities for theatrical production waned, she turned to writing political fiction and narratives. She died in 1689, the year after the Roman Catholic James II was replaced by the Protestant William and Mary, but she maintained her stance as a supporter of James II to the last. We even have some striking small details, such as her complaint to the bookseller Tonson about penury after the theatres closed. But we do not know very much. Many more questions about Behn's life remain unanswered. Did she love women as well as men? Did she marry? Did she go to Surinam? Was she a Roman Catholic? Some of these questions may be answered, more or less equivocally, in time. For the present, however, we know too little about her life to read her writings confidently against it. And what we do know is often mediated by the interpretation of contemporaries.

When she was alive Behn was an object of fascination. She was abused and attacked for her success on the stage, showing that she was seen as a force to be reckoned with. She also had a reputation for sexual freedom – or certainly for writing with freedom about sexual issues – which led to a decline in her reputation during the eighteenth century. The information we have about Behn is not – as in the case of, say, Charles Dickens's letters – that of a life which is in part private, in part public, but is more complicated. On the one hand, as one biographer points out, Behn's life offers a 'sheer lack of [the] intimate detail which biographies...have led us to expect'.[3] On the other hand she is used as an inceptionary figure in women's literary production. This renders Behn the site of intense biographical speculation. So, despite the lack of information, most scholarly work on Behn has been broadly biographical, and this has sometimes meant taking the writings as evidence about her character and life.

Critical emphasis on Behn as speaking for women, both as a 'first' (as a professional) and as their representative, is helpful in giving us a way to focus on her, but is also problematic in obscuring the specific influences upon her, especially the way in which her texts appeared in commercial genres and were therefore linked to the dominant ideologies represented in those genres. Angeline Goreau sums up the position which sees Behn as a first when she writes that 'Mrs Behn imposed herself on history without precedent: she was the first woman to become a professional writer. Aphra had to invent herself'; and – if Behn had not managed – 'we would have had to invent her'.[4]

That Behn is the first woman to earn her living by her pen is something on which almost all the biographers focus, so that she has become something of an icon as the 'first professional woman writer'. This characterization tends not to explore the implicit contradictions between the commercialism implied by the term 'professional writer' and the authenticity conjured up by the term 'woman writer'. In taking up Behn as a first, critics both follow the lead of Virginia Woolf in *A Room of One's Own* but suppress some of the implications of Woolf's emphasis on the commercial nature of Behn's writing. As well as indicating Behn's exceptional status as a woman professional, Woolf noted that Behn, working 'on equal terms with men', produced commercial texts in the dominant genres. She even claims that the very fact that Behn wrote commercially 'outweighs anything that she actually wrote', because it paves the way for 'freedom of the mind' for women.[5] Woolf's emphasis on the commercial alerts us to that contradiction between an authentic female voice implied in the use of Behn as an iconic woman writer, and the commercial and ideological demands of professional writing in commercial genres.

This contradictory emphasis on Behn as both woman writer and professional can be avoided. Rather than take Behn as an iconic figure of the first woman professional and attempt to assimilate our understandings of her texts to that fixed, but self-contradictory, point, we can take up the questions of genre, status, politics, and gender raised by the texts she produced and their relationship to circumstances. Of course, it does help to know things about Behn. But it is possible to resist the temptation to explain the texts by turning to the life because, in the end, our idea of Behn's life, or our idea of her as a 'first professional woman', has as much fictional material in it as any other story. To explain a text by details from a life in any literal way is to explain fiction by myth. As Jacqueline Rose has argued with regard to

Sylvia Plath, another author who has generated a critical and biographical industry based on projection, these 'accounts of the life... have to base themselves on a spurious claim to knowledge, they have to arbitrate between competing and often incompatible versions of what took place'.[6]

RESTORATION POLITICS

Any attempt to situate Behn's texts in historical contexts immediately produces a sense of the centrality of political discourses and conflicts throughout her career. However, it is impossible to do more than sketch the political complexity of the period from the 1660s to 1689. If Behn was born in 1640, this was just before the Civil War began, culminating, after different kinds of struggle, in the declaration of the English republic in 1649 after Charles I was beheaded. In 1653 the republic collapsed and Oliver Cromwell became Protector. In 1660 Charles II was restored to the throne. While this was far from the end of republican theory and insurrection, it came to pose a new problem, generally known as the Exclusion Crisis.[7] When it became clear that Charles II would have no heir and his brother James, Duke of York, was a Roman Catholic, attempts were made by the Commons and others to exclude Catholics from the succession and, by some, to institute a favoured but illegitimate Protestant son of the king, James, Duke of Monmouth, as the heir. These issues bubbled to the surface around the so-called Popish Plot 'disclosed' by Titus Oates in 1678, creating a sequence of attacks first on Catholics and then on republicans. By 1681 many feared another civil war. From about 1681 the terms 'Whig' and 'Tory' came to be generally used to designate those respectively questioning and supporting the succession of James, Duke of York. Many fled, and when Charles II died in 1685 Monmouth led a rebellion in the West Country, for which he was executed in 1686. James II became king, but in 1688 he was deposed in the so-called Glorious Revolution; and the Protestant William and Mary became rulers.

Behn seems to have been in the thick of all this. Her writing, although fascinated by the Civil War period which it circles and reworks, was often published as polemic in the pro-Stuart cause. So, while Behn remains unusual in being a woman in this sphere, she is far from being a self-created woman writer for her texts can be seen as actively participating in the dominant political and literary discourses of her period, as her poetry suggests.

WHY READ BEHN?

This Introduction argues, in part, that we cannot simply see Behn as an author in the sense of someone who produces a unified corpus of material. Her work is constantly marked by generic and commercial contingencies, and the nature of the work she produced makes it hard to locate a 'real' Aphra Behn. She registers and comments upon the political, sexual, and financial ideologies of the time; but just as she seems to support the ability of women to articulate and pursue their desires in some texts, in others such activities are condemned. She writes novels that turn into romances, and vice versa. While she is clearly a fervent supporter of Charles II and James II, her poetry and long fiction *Love Letters between a Nobleman and his Sister* betray a fascination with James Duke of Monmouth and with Commonwealth.

With regard to *Oroonoko*, particularly, we are provoked to ask whether the contradictions are in Behn's writing or in the ideological contradictions of the moment at which she wrote. Of course, in the case of *Oroonoko* and the other texts too, the answer is both. And this paradoxical position is why we should read Behn. We do not need to agree with her position on James II or on questions of marriage and separation. Indeed, even in the apparently straightforward sphere of Tory politics her texts are paradoxical in their fixation on the political 'other'. They speak to us about questions of desire, gender, and power which still interest and motivate us; but they speak in a way which articulates the contradictions inherent in the historical moment from which, as Jürgen Habermas has argued, we can see the lineaments of modernity emerging. In the oppositions of Behn's texts we can trace not only some of the contradictions on which the Enlightenment and post-Enlightenment state is founded, but also the emergence of a debate *about* the state, a contradictory literary-political commentary, critique, and debate which Habermas has called the 'bourgeois public sphere'. This sphere is not an orderly place of loquacious debate, but a market place of opinions and desires which also circulate as commodities and in which literary and other cultural texts circulate to readers. This sphere of commentary, intermingling the political and commercial, is inhabited by Behn's texts; we can read them for their rich contradictions rather than their coherences and certainties. The Behn in the chapters which follow is one whose writings both embody the contradictions of society and, at the same time, offer a critique of it. As texts emerging at a crucial moment in modernity, they pose problems that were all important when she wrote: of the nature and authority of the state, of desire, marriage, money, and language.

2

Poetry

BEHN AS A RESTORATION POET

Before we can begin to ask what kind of poet Behn was, it is necessary to investigate the ways in which poetry was produced in the period. The conditions of literary production during the Restoration were such that poems might circulate in a variety of forms, from copied manuscript to printed anthology. This meant that poems might exist in several different versions, and can be misattributed. Scholars are still in doubt about whether some poems are by Behn or by other contemporaries. That *her* poems were recirculated and copied, and that some poems now attributed to her were claimed for other poets, are marks of her integration into the mainstream of London literary production, and not, as it might seem to us now, 'the fate of the woman writer'.[1]

When Behn was writing, poetry was not considered to be a medium for the expression of feelings (as some people have regarded it in the twentieth century). Although poetry might address personal issues, it was more often considered to be a shared and public discourse. Thus, while in the nineteenth century an elegy would probably be a personal poem about a dead person, and expressive of a poet's feelings, in the seventeenth century, as Milton's 'Lycidas' and Behn's elegy for Rochester suggest, even an elegy would be the occasion of other thoughts and a public manipulation of the codes of a particular type of poem. One indication of how meanings change is that in the seventeenth century an elegy did not have to be about a dead person at all.

Much verse was occasional in the sense of being written in relation to specific events – whether public, political, scandalous, or social. Such poetry was a form of commentary on and intervention

10

in social and political events and opinions. Moreover, during the last quarter of the seventeenth century print was an increasingly important mode for public commentary taking a variety of forms. Newspapers had been circulating since the 1620s and became fully established during the Civil War. Broadsides and short pamphlets flourished during times of crisis. Ballads, as well as books, were printed and hung up in inns or circulated in coffee-houses where popular opinion was formed. Manuscript satires were copied and circulated, and in the 1680s there seems to have been an industry of hand-copying the latest poems and lampoons for sale. Poems were pirated, and editions of poems were collected in miscellanies, often anonymously. Behn's poem 'The Disappointment', for example, first appeared in a pirated volume of poems by the Earl of Rochester.[2] It is clear that contemporaries were interested in who wrote which poems; but, even for them, it was not always clear. Even a contemporary attribution of a poem to a particular poet might not be as simple as an assertion of authorship – the evidence is often complicated by political or personal investments and, in the case of women writers, it was sometimes claimed that men must have written their work.

Information about Behn's authorship of poems comes from a variety of sources. Only in the case of 'On the Death of E. Waller Esq.' is there a manuscript in her hand. Other information comes from early eighteenth-century reprints, from assertions, and from attributions in books in which she was involved as translator, contributor, or editor. Behn may well have compiled *Covent Garden Drolery* (1672), a fashionable volume whose second edition is marked 'A.B.'. In 1684 *Poems on Several Occasions: With a Voyage to the Island of Love* appeared containing poems and translations by Behn. In 1685 *Miscellany, Being a collection of Poems By several Hands* included some of her poems, poems addressed to her, and her translation of La Rochefoucauld's maxims as 'Seneca Unmasqued'. Her last collection, including poems by others, was *Lycidus... Together with a Miscellany of New Poems By Several Hands* (1688),[3] and her poetry also appeared in collections, most notably in *Poems on Several Occasions* (1673). Finally, 'Astraea's Book', a manuscript book of the satirical verse of the 1680s, exists in several hands, one of which may well be Behn's.

As Janet Todd has argued, Behn's poetic output is an object lesson in the varied and commercial engagement of literary genre and market. The poems range from political ballads (for example, the ballads 'to a Scotch tune' on the career of Charles II's illegitimate son, James, Duke of Monmouth), through occasional pieces and translations, to pastoral, amorous, and erotic verse.[4] Despite this generic diversity, I have chosen to divide Behn's poetry into 'political' and 'amorous' topics and associated genres. These two spheres often overlap, as in 'Ovid to Julia', attributed to Behn, where a court love-affair signifies in both political and erotic terms. However, it is possible to examine the genres of panegyric, ballad, and satire in relation to specifically political or amorous topics. (Behn's Tory reworking of Aesop's fables has been omitted because of lack of space). The most important link between her political and sexual poetry is their shared attitude to poetic rhetoric as providing a power, albeit retrospective and qualified, to control the reader's understanding of a situation and therefore its political, ideological, and moral value. An understanding of poetry as meditating on this power of language to represent – and persuade – runs through Behn's political and amorous poetry.

POLITICAL POETRY

The power of political poetry, especially in commercial market relations rather than those of patronage, is to persuade, thereby ensuring its own circulation and the currency of its opinions. Behn's political poetry included royal panegyric (poems of praise), satirical attacks on other commentators, ballads, fables, satirical epistles, and poems written to commemorate particular occasions. She employed the main political genres and addressed the same central political issues as other Tory poets of the period. The rhetoric of these poems makes clear that in an ideal situation the best – most eloquent and persuasive – language ought to coincide with the best, or 'true', political ideas; and therefore her political poetry can be read in part as offering a continuing commentary on the uses and ends of eloquence.

In Behn's praise of Charles II and especially of the Roman Catholic James II, who succeeded Charles to the throne despite serious parliamentary and public opposition, her poems elaborate a complex symbolic discourse supporting the rule of the Stuart

12

dynasty. James II is presented as a peacekeeper amongst rebels, one 'To whom the great Command was giv'n | The first born *Rebells* to chastise' ('A Pindaric...Coronation', Todd, i. 201. 31–5). The language of compliment was thus an active intervention in political debates.

However, the attempt to persuade a larger audience was central to more populist genres, such as the political ballad. Using this form, Behn returned several times to the ill-fated career of Charles II's son, James, Duke of Monmouth, who as a popular hero and object of political speculation invited satire. Behn's ballads are addressed to an implicitly slightly critical, popular audience. In the use of catchy populist forms, political implications are woven into easy tunes in such a way that message and medium become equally simple and therefore seem obviously to be 'true'. Such ballads intervened in the political situation at a relatively popular level. They did so by mimicking the folkloric simplicity of the simple (and implicitly politically innocent) ballad. 'Silvio's Complaint: A Song, To a Fine Scotch Tune', for example, has a chorus commenting on Monmouth's political ambitions.

> A Noble Youth but all Forlorn,
> Lig'd Sighing by a Spring:
> 'Twere better I's was nere Born,
> Ere wisht to be a King.

> (Todd, i. 82. 5–8)

Despite the apparent structural simplicity of this ballad, printed in *Poems on Several Occasions* (1684), when Monmouth's fortunes were at a low ebb, it deals with political issues in a characteristically complex way. The expression of political commentary and condemnation in ballad form, which suggests an inevitability rather than agency about Monmouth's attempt to take power, is reinforced by the pastoral mode, recasting potentially cynical politics in terms of innocence and fate. For the reader it does not offer a simple invitation to condemn Silvio's attempts to gain political power, but suggests a persuasive account of Silvio as a victim of a political struggle in which his failure, though posed as inescapable (and implicitly deserved), also has claims on the reader's sympathy.

The coincidence of eloquent political rhetoric with a good cause is reformulated by Behn's fables and satires.[5] The satire 'To Poet

13

Bavius' contains an attack on the ambitions of her opponents. The poet John Baber is abused for his faint praise of the birth of James II's child, for attacking some of James II's policies, and for his ill-wrought lines, 'Produc'd ... without Thinking or Design':

> And had not thy Unlucky *Rhiming Spirit*,
> Writ *Satyr* now, instead of *Panegyrick*:
> Vile Pointless *Satyr*, thou might'st still have been
> A poor forgotten Drone without a Sting.

(Todd, i. 299. 36–9)

The 'Drone without a Sting' involves an association, found also elsewhere in Behn, between eloquence and masculinity.

A final piece of evidence for the suitability of eloquence to the best causes can be found at the very end of Behn's career in her 'Pindaric Poem to the Reverend Doctor Burnet'. Burnet was an eminent Anglican, now best known for his gossipy *History of his Own Times*. After the so-called 'Glorious Revolution', in which the Roman Catholic James II was banished and the Protestant William and Mary came to rule in England, he attempted to enlist Behn's pen in their support. Behn's poem in response takes the occasion of a polite refusal of his invitation, to expose the relationship between rhetoric and power, on the one hand, and rhetoric and truth, on the other. The poem oscillates between the languages of political and erotic persuasion by using the analogy of a lover's attempt on his mistress's virtue as a figure for Burnet's attempt at political 'seduction'. This figure also organizes the power relations of the poem in terms of masculine power and 'persuasive force' versus woman's silence and virtue. However, as the extract below makes clear, by playing on its own disempowered virtue versus Burnet's power the poem usurps the very persuasive eloquence which it attributes to Burnet. The self-representation of the speaker as speaking involuntarily, like Echo (described by the critic John Hollander as 'a voice-activated device, unable to originate discourse, unable to forbear from reply'), gestures towards the poem's speaker's female status but also towards the poem's political echo of the past.[6] The abandoned and voiceless nymph is apparently able only 'to Sigh with Echo', but the poem uses the covert power of the manipulation of former sounds (a reference to Behn's praise of James II) to subvert and change Burnet's words:

14

A thousand ways my Soul you can Invade,
And spight of my Opinions weak Defence,
  Against my Will, you Conquer and Perswade.
Your language, soft as Love, betrays the Heart,
  And at each Period fixes a Resistless Dart,
While the fond Listener, like a Maid undone,
  Inspir'd with Tenderness she fears to own;
In vain essays her Freedom to Regain.

(Todd, i. 308. 1–16)

By describing politics as a sexual siege involving unfair power
relations, the poem undermines the imagined persuasions of
Burnet and invites the reader to sympathize with the true, but
suppressed, voice and sentiments of the speaker. The presentation
of Burnet as a seductive rhetorician who must be resisted permits
the subversive employment of a chain of analogies; for instance,
the word 'conquer', habitually borrowed from the language of
war by the poetry of courtship, is here redeployed in a political
poem so that both its implications are active for the reader. The
analogy of seduction implies the persona's involuntary attach-
ment to virtue, like that of a chaste mistress, but combines this
with political virtue. In its complex negotiation of the power of
storytelling and voice with its interweaving of contrasting
discourses, the poem draws on associations between power and
eloquence found also in Behn's poems on amorous topics.

AMOROUS POETRY

The manipulation of eloquence, and its qualified power to give an
account of events with which the speaker might well be otherwise
powerless, is also foregrounded in Behn's amorous verse. Much of
this amorous poetry uses and reworks the forms and topics of the
love poetry of the period in relation to feminine desire.

Other women poets of the period, too, were reworking poetic
forms. One of them was Katherine Philips, known as the 'chaste
Orinda', a royalist poet who came to prominence in the early
years of the Restoration with her translations and poems. Philips
turned the discourse of courtly love towards the poetry of
friendship, so that a poem entitled *Injuria amici* begins in the same
way as a lover's lament – 'lovely apostate! what was my

offence? I Or am I punished for obedience?'[7] Behn shares with Philips and other poets such as Ann Finch, Countess of Winchelsea, a highly self-conscious understanding of the relationship between gender and poetic genre. Like Philips and Finch, Behn used contemporary versions of pastoral poetry (set in Arcadia, an idealized rural landscape inhabited by the shepherds of literary convention). And like other poets, Behn adapted genres which tend to assume a male speaking voice, such as the quasi-Petrarchan discourse which habitually used comparisons to articulate a relationship between the speaking voice and an object, as in 'Shall I compare thee to a summer's day?'. However, she also wrote in the libertine discourse which not only took as its object various kinds of sexual activities, but was also in a highly ambivalent relation to the high valuation placed on female chastity in poems of courtly love.

Indeed, like the famous libertine John Wilmot, Earl of Rochester, Behn wrote the kind of poem called the 'imperfect enjoyment', on the topic of premature ejaculation or impotence. Here the reader's expectations are generated by a libertine discourse where masculinity, sexual desire, and poetic potency are associated. Hence, while other women poets such as Katherine Philips were seen as virtuous – 'Virtue (dear Friend) needs no defence', wrote the Earl of Roscommon to Philips – Behn's reputation during the century after her death was determined in part by critical condemnation of her use of the libertine discourse in poetry and her representation of sexual desire in poetry, plays, and fiction.[8]

A complex account of sexual and literary power is found in Behn's elegy 'On the Death of the Late Earl of Rochester'. This became part of an exchange between Behn and another poet, Rochester's niece Ann Wharton, about moral (rather than poetic) decorum in relation to gender and poetry. The elegy mourns Rochester's early death; but, paradoxically, it also tends to point to the female poet's voice outliving his. And it becomes the occasion for an analysis of poetic power through the way in which Rochester is commemorated. Far from condemning his libertinage, the elegy calls upon all those who would mourn the poet: the Muses, but also 'all ye little Gods of Love, whose Darts, I Have lost their wonted power of piercing hearts', and lovers (apparently female):

Mourn, all ye Beauties, put your *Cyprus* on,
The truest Swain that e're Ador'd you's gone;
Think how he lov'd, and writ, and sigh'd, and spoke,
Recall his Meen, his Fashion, and his Look.
By what dear Arts the Soul he did surprize,
Soft as his Voice, and charming as his Eyes.

(Todd, i. 162. 23–40)

The elegy proposes an interrelationship of erotic power and poetic eloquence, suggested in the simultaneously poetic and sexual significances of 'Look' and 'Voice'. The ambiguous term 'ador'd', which could refer to poetic or physical homage, initiates the elision of poetic and erotic power in these six lines, a mixing facilitated by the use of the rhyming couplet as a very compressed unit of sense. The 'Beauties' are to mourn, perhaps, because Rochester's death deprives them of the poetic 'Arts' which did 'the soul...surprize'; but these 'dear Arts' might imply sexual as much as literary pleasuring. Moreover, the eyes of the poet are invoked as the masculine lover's gaze in Petrarchan poetry, and Rochester, while presented in terms of the power of the masculine gaze ('his Look') is also shown as speaking ('and sigh'd, and spoke', 'Soft as his Voice') – an activity even more ambivalently poised between poetic lover and poet. Through the interweaving of compliment to erotic and poetic mastery encoded in a sharing of terms, the elegy memorializes Rochester by building up a discourse which fuses erotic (masculine) and poetic power.

Poetic power remains analogous to masculine erotic power, figured as penetrative; it finds out and points meaning for the reader as Cupid's darts point out love. Ann Wharton, related to Rochester and herself a poet, responded to this entangling of sexual and poetic power by suggesting that Behn eschew the libertine aspect of poetry associated with Rochester and 'bid your Muse maintain a Vestal Fire', so that she might have 'Sappho's...wit without her Shame'.[9] As Wharton had noticed, for all its many forms, Behn's poetry acts as a stage in which dramas of gender and desire are played out with the greatest concentration.

Rather than taking up Ann Wharton's suggestion, Behn's poetry – pastoral, quasi-Petrarchan, and libertine – investigates feminine desire and the power of language. In 'On Desire. A Pindarick' (published in 1688), in the translation from Ovid's 'A Paraphrase on Oenone to Paris' (first published in 1680), and in

17

'Voyage to the Island of Love', a translation of Abbé Paul Tallemant's *Voyage de l'Isle d'Amour* (1663) published in *Poems Upon Several Occasions* (1684), Behn takes up the problems of feminine desire since the passing of the golden age and the arrival of highly gendered models of love and poetry whose strictures work against feminine satisfaction.

In her translation of the fifth letter in Ovid's *Heroides* which appeared in *Ovid's Epistles Translated by Several Hands* (1680), prefaced by Dryden, the nymph Oenone, deserted by Paris, tells her own story of extreme feminine powerlessness. She presents herself as the innocent victim both of fate and man in alliance, and all too vulnerable because betrayed by her own eyes: 'at thy sight the kindling Fire would rise, I And I, unskil'd, declare it at my eyes' (Todd, i. 13. 44–5). Her single, innocent, and undisguised love is likened to 'hidden Treasure long conceal'd', an economic metaphor which implies a contrast between sexual and affective thrift versus reckless disbursement. As such she is an easy victim for the seductive but deceitful rhetoric of her beloved: 'Quick to my Heart the perjur'd Accents ran, I Which I took in, believ'd, and was undone' (Todd, i. 13. 60–1); and she ends the poem still longing for his return. Thus 'Love', or longing, for Paris renders her incapacitated and immobile. Literally stranded on an island, she is only able to assert her position by her description of the situation, which includes a prophecy: 'a wrong'd Husband does thy [Paris's] Death design'. The lament of Oenone is typical of one aspect of feminine desire in Behn's poetry, in which desire is dangerous, even fatal, to women – as was suggested in the poem to Burnet. Like that poem, 'Oenone' presents feminine desire as likely to lead to disaster. But it implicitly sets this against other forms of power, such as that of telling the story.

Desire is once again presented as a disaster for the woman in Behn's translation of 'Voyage to the Island of Love'. This is a much longer poem, apparently analysing desire, courtship, and 'conquest' from the point of view of the male lover, Lisander, who tells the story of his love for Aminta to his friend. The poem can be seen as a kind of secular *Pilgrim's Progress*, in that most of it is taken up with Lisander calling at various places ('Inquietude', 'The River of Despair', 'Jealousy') on his way to the consummation of his love in the final section, called 'The Prospect and Bower of Bliss'. Behn as translator expands the original poem in two sections, both of which deal with the connection of death with desire for Aminta. First, in 'The Truce', a section is inserted to tell us that Lisander, the lover, is recounting the story of his love for Aminta when she is dead – *'Forget'*, he tells himself, *'thou saw'st the lovely yielding Maid, I Dead in thy trembling Arms'* – ensuring that one question which the English reader brings to the translated text is, *how* did poor Aminta die? The second expanded and transformed section is the final one on the consummation of desire and its associated catastrophe.[10] In the bower, 'Recesses dark, and Grottoes all conspire, I *To favour Love and soft desire'* (Todd, i. 155. 2051) in one of Behn's favoured pastoral settings; and the section ends with an expansion and reworking of the French original.

The poem puts the encounter in the language of courtly love, whereby sexual intercourse is articulated as 'conquest'. Paradoxically, the section opens with a (temporary) loss of sexual power, a kind of death, on Lisander's part, figured as premature ejaculation – a topic used significantly elsewhere by Behn, and one which formed the central issue of the Restoration libertine poems of 'imperfect enjoyment':

> A while all Dead between her Arms I lay,
> Unable to possess the conquer'd Joys;
> But by degrees my Soul its sense retriev'd;
> Shame and Confusion let me know I liv'd.
> I saw the trembling dis-appointed Maid,
> With charming angry Eyes my fault up-braid.
>
> (Todd, i. 156. 2081–6)

Although he has 'conquer'd', he has failed to 'possess' fully, suggesting that full 'possession' includes penetration and perhaps the sharing of pleasure. Masculine power in love is exposed as contingent rather than absolute. This *petit mort* qualifies the supremacy of the lover who has – after more than two thousand lines – finally seduced his mistress. The language indicates the vulnerability of masculine sexual power ('possess', 'conquer'd') when 'love' requires the mutuality of pleasure ('Joys', 'charming angry Eyes', 'fault').

Yet this loss of power lasts only for a moment and, it turns out, prefigures the death of the nymph which the audience has been alerted to expect. Where premature orgasm temporarily castrates Lisander, sexual pleasure kills Aminta. During an erotic encounter in the bower she dies – still beautiful, as Death 'not one Beauty did surprize' – and, adoring, she calls him a 'blessing too extream to be possest'. The fading of masculine passion after 'conquest' is here replaced by a violent erasure of the woman at the moment of pleasure; her 'fleeting soul as quickly disappears' after erotic contact rather than passion fading and desire seeking a new object. Thus the poem resolves the problem that 'conquest' produces disappointment and a moving-on of desire to a new object by brutally foreshortening any narrative of abandonment: it end-stops desire with death at the moment of fulfilment. For the reader, the final part of the poem offers a forceful stopping of the story of desire. But precisely *because* Aminta dies, the encounter is complete and self-contained, and therefore offers a scenario which could be repeated. (The reader may wish to compare this with the end of *Oroonoko*). Although the whole poem is set within the framework of her death, it is by no means elegiac; rather, it is an anatomy of desire. And, as the term 'anatomy' suggests, it offers a complete overview of the endlessly repeated experience of desire, closed to form one complete unit of a repeated story. Thus, the 'fading' of passion, so often analysed in Behn's writing, is transferred to death of the Maid:

> I Kiss and Bathe her stiffening Face with Tears,
> Press it to mine, as cold and pale as hers;
> The fading Roses of her lips I press.

> (Todd, i. 158. 2157–9)

The completeness of the experience, its closed-off quality, is symbolized by the construction of a 'monument' by Lisander from which he can see in 'Prospect' the whole landscape of desire – the route travelled to the 'conquest' of Aminta. Thus, the landscape of desire has been objectified and known by the masculine lover, here, at the cost of the death of the woman.

Questions of control over desire and over narration recur continually in Behn's poetry, in elegies, pastoral, and in her work in libertine genres. She examines the significance of premature ejaculation in a way which both continues and contrasts with other (male) writers who use the topic. The nymph in *Voyage* is figured as responding to lost pleasure as does the beloved in Rochester's 'The Imperfect Enjoyment', where, 'Smiling, she chides ... And from her Body wipes the clammy joys ... is there no more? I She cries'. Moreover, *Voyage* shares the witty representation of sexual courtship

of Rochester, or Etherege's version of the genre. Etherege is careful
to note that the woman is struggling against her own desires, not
brute force: 'She does resist my Love with a pleasing force; I Mov'd
not with Anger, but with Modesty.' The difference in Behn's
treatment is in the exploration of the consequences of desire.

Behn's 'The Disappointment' indicates the distinct points of
view of men and women, hinting at the tangle of moral and erotic
difficulty caused for women when, in Etherege's terms, a man's
'Zeal does [his] Devotion quite destroy'; and it elaborates the
serious implications for a woman who 'fails' to resist desire.[11]
Where Rochester's and Etherege's poems broadly take the man's
point of view implicit in their shared title 'The Imperfect
Enjoyment', Behn, as the title 'The Disappointment' suggests,
offers a version of the incident complicated by its indication that
there are two perspectives involved. The 'nymph' has been *both*
'conquered' and *also* disappointed by desire. Thus, where 'none
can guess *Lysander's* Soul', when he is 'Damn'd... to the Hell of
Impotence', the poem does offer to speak for her – 'The *Nymph's*
Resentments none but I [the narrator, implicitly female
here] I Can well Imagine or Condole'. Thus the genre is
reworked in such a way as to be told in part from the point of
view of the woman who, her honour betrayed by desire, and
further betrayed by disappointment, 'flies'. However, despite this
flight, the narrating voice does retell the story and therefore to an
extent recuperate her point of view.

Feminine desire figures in other Behn poems as an uncontrol-
lable psychic force, dangerous to both the woman herself and
social forms. In 'On Desire: A Pindarick' the speaker asks:

> Where wert thou, oh, malicious spright,
> When shining Honour did invite?
>
> .   .   .   .   .
>
> When thou cou'dst mix ambition with my joy,
> Then peevish *Phäntôm* thou wer't nice and coy.
>
> (Todd, i. 281–2, 24–31)

Thus, desire is repeatedly narrated by Behn's poetry as a force
beyond the control of the female subject.

However, if desire is described as causing damage to and
possibly complete annihilation of subjectivity in the female, the
power of poetry and especially of narration, or the power to 'tell

the story', figures in her writing as a partially compensatory ability. Even Oenone, who has lost her love utterly, is able to *tell* the story; and this, as Rosalind Ballaster indicates, suggests the importance of the position and covert power of the narrator in Behn's texts, both poetic and fictional.[12] Behn is famous for having referred to poetry as her 'masculine part': if poetry and 'telling' are 'masculine' – for Behn, connoting power – then in her poetry the powerlessness of feminine desire is to an extent counterbalanced by the ability to *tell*. To summarize: sexual and rhetorical potency are set against each other, to some extent in a compensatory manner, in many of her poems on female desire. The power of narration to which many of the poems call attention – like 'The Disappointment', 'Desire', even 'Oenone', though not 'Voyage to the Island of Love' – follow such a pattern.

A poetic narration, to an extent, recuperates the depredations of desire. The power of narration to control representation and meaning is noticeable – for instance, in 'On the First Discovery of Falseness in Amintas', when the abandoned nymph plans to go to a grove and die, but not before telling the story – 'But dying, breath thyself out a tale'.

The paradox of desire as a remover of control, and the power of language to tell its story, are given an additional twist in 'To Damon. *To Inquire of him if he cou'd tell me by the Style, who writ me a Copy of Verses that came to me in an Unknown Hand*'. Here the receipt of verses provokes desire which immediately turns to representation and recounting – we are told of the subject's imaginary painting of the sender of the verses as a perfect man. In this poem, the emphasis is placed on the *subject's* ability to create the object of desire and tell the story. The poem is spoken in a female voice which describes her state: though 'Free as the Air, and calm as that', she finds it dull. The arrival of the verses, then, disrupts a tedium ready to be disrupted; and although it is described in the usual terms of the invasion of her heart by masculine desire 'My Heart was by my Eyes misled'), the verses are also viewed with an ironic detachment with regard to discourses of courtship, since they are described as 'fill'd with praises of my face and eyes, I My verse, and all the usual flatteries I To me as common as the Air'. Moreover, they prompt her own imagination to invent a perfect man as the sender, thus displacing purely masculine control of the occasion:

by the Soul, I drew the Swain.
Charming as fancy cou'd create
Fine as his Poem, and soft as that.
I drew him all the heart cou'd move
I drew him all that women Love.
And such a dear Idea made
As has my whole repose betray'd.
Pigmalion thus his image form'd,
And for the charms he made, he sigh'd and burn'd.

(Todd, i. 271. 80–88)

The image is created by the speaker and explained to the reader in terms of the myth of Pygmalion, in which a sculptor first created the image of his desire, desired, and then brought the image to life. But Behn's text reverses the genders, and creative power is usurped by the usually gazed-upon female speaker.

Thus creative power, the power both to describe the imagined perfect man and to narrate and ironize the incident, making it into a story of the figuring of female desire in female invention – 'I drew', 'a dear Idea made' – emphatically rests with the narrator. In this poem, any sense of the masculine power of conquest is substantially undercut by the female speaker's ability to imagine and recount; and Pygmalion is presented as sighing and burning. But the poem also calls attention to the way the speaker actually *invents* the very object which, elsewhere in the poems, is seen as damaging the subject by causing desire. The object of desire, rather than being an independent force that damages the female subject, is cunningly represented as – in itself – her invention.

This trick is recapitulated in a different way in 'To the fair Clarinda, *who made Love to me, imagin'd more than Woman*', which, as Ballaster notes, sets up a 'complex play of gendered subjectivity' whereby we are made aware of the ability of the narrating voice to create the object of desire as doubly gendered. The poem creates for us an unresolved conundrum of gender which remains in the final line, 'The Love to Hermes, Aphrodite the Friend', maintaining the paradox in the figure of the hermaphrodite.[13] The existence of the object of desire which acts upon and is also created by the lover/ speaker is central here as a paradox of desire sustainable by the very act of telling. As a story it does not require a simplistic reduction to one of mere gender, but can maintain paradoxical opposites of meaning and representation.

We can trace in Behn's poetry an oscillation between an emphasis on the annihilation of the female subject caused by sexual desire and its social implications, and the very power of telling to reconstruct the scene. Her poetry offers a complex and contradictory account of the power of desire and of the political and amorous power of eloquence; and, as we have seen, its spectrum covers formal panegyric to libertine lyric, offering contradictory accounts of the place of women in relation to eloquence and power.

The interrelationship between gender, sexuality, and power was played out in a rather different way in Behn's texts for the Restoration theatre, and it is to these genres and institutions that she made her earliest commercial contributions. Her output for the theatre resembled her career in poetry in that it was not restricted to the acceptable female genres. Indeed, in theatre there *were* no commercial genres which were unequivocally acceptable for female writers. And Behn wrote polemical comedies that, like her poems, interweave sexuality and politics. These are explored in the next chapter.

3

Plays

THE RESTORATION STAGE

Behn's career as a dramatist runs through the 1670s and 1680s. What kind of stage did she write for? What conditions and expectations faced a woman writer working in one of the most public and commercial areas of literary production? What social and cultural place did the theatre inhabit? As these questions suggest, before we look closely at Behn's comedies it is essential to have some understanding of the specific conditions of the Restoration stage.

The theatre in which Behn worked was an institution reconstituted and transformed after the closure of the theatres during the period of the English Civil War and Protectorate between 1642 and 1660. The Restoration theatres had been set up by Charles II in 1660, when he decreed that the London theatres should be organized by two patent companies run by Sir Thomas Killigrew and Sir William Davenant. They were located at two theatres, the King's and the Duke's, and the repertoire of plays from before the Civil War was divided between them. The fact that the King himself went regularly to the theatre, instead of having plays brought to court, set the fashion for theatre-going as a social activity of some importance. However, the politicization of theatre during the Civil War and Protectorate also had a crucial effect on the early Restoration stage: plays regularly recapitulated and reworked the events of the Civil War and Protectorate, though habitually in response to the political events of their own time.

Restoration modes of staging facilitated a close and complex relationship between audience and play. One of its novelties was the employment of actresses, who were used to provide the audience with the twin pleasures of the role actually played and the erotic spectacle of the actress herself. The theatres also utilized

25

a wide range of staging devices which permitted movement between illusionistic theatre and the breaking of the frame by actors and audience, giving an enhanced illusionistic sense of a spectator entering a world with a range of different scenes and interiors, and using sliding scenery to reveal scenes and to make 'discoveries'; this is explored in the next section (see pp. 46–7). On the other hand, the plays began and ended with prologues and epilogues, spoken by actors and often written by friends of the dramatist, which carefully mediated between play and audience (the fact that Behn wrote many prologues and epilogues is testimony to her central position in this world). The forestage offered playing spaces close to the audience, facilitating exchanges between its members and the actors. 'Characters' on the Restoration stage were not hermetically sealed fictions: the role might be broken by an actor in asides, or work metatheatrically to make reference to the audience or to the act of playing itself.

Of about 400 plays written between 1660 and 1700, a fairly large proportion were comedies, or plays using a comic or tragicomic mode. Behn wrote both tragicomedies (which mixed tragic potential with comic outcome) and comedies, but only one tragedy – the emotive *Abdelazar* (1676). Behn's comedies of intrigue (apart from *The Rover* and the exceptional *The Widow Ranter*) tended to be set in London and to be 'city' comedies in that they dealt with urban life and presented political, gender, and economic struggle in an urban setting similar to that inhabited by their audience. Her tragicomedies of the 1670s and later 1680s, however, use a different kind of plotting and foreign setting. *The False Count* and *The Dutch Lover* are both tragicomedies, which John Loftis argues are influenced by Spanish plays of the period. In each play the plot offers an apparently insoluble problem, such as love between siblings. The audience, familiar with tragicomic conventions, might spend the first four acts enjoying a particularly tortuous and improbable problem and waiting for the surprise resolution. In *The Dutch Lover*, for instance, a resolution is provided by the disclosure of concealed information in a recognition scene. Politico-sexual comedies, on the other hand, tend to resolve plots not by disclosure, but by the resolution of sexual, economic, and political situations in favour of protagonists who are themselves the agents of change.

Comedy, however, was regarded as one of the lower, populist

forms: in 1671 Dryden commented that comedy was 'in its own nature, inferior to all sorts of dramatic writing. Low comedy especially requires, on the writer's part, much conversation with the vulgar.' Dryden implied that not only was comedy a low genre, pointing out the faults in low people and manners, but also the practitioners were likely to be conversant themselves with such manners, unlike the producers of the high-flown sentiments of tragedy.[1] Laughter itself was seen as a problematic response. Repeating the texts of Greek writers, Thomas Hobbes wrote of laughter as 'a passion that hath *no name*; but the sign of it is that distortion of the countenance which we call laughter'.[2] Increasingly, it came to be undignified for a gentleman to grimace or twist his face in laughter; yet, inevitably, laughter was part of the complex unruliness of the Restoration audience.

The average size of a London theatre audience during Behn's career has been estimated at about 500, and although the gallants and, later, political factions are the dominant voices in this audience as recorded in surviving documents, a wide spectrum of society was present either in the audience or working at the playhouse. Women were present for their own pleasure and in an economic capacity as actresses, prostitutes, and orange-sellers. Men could include the nobility, from Charles II downwards (for example, both Charles II and his brother James, Duke of York, later James II, attended Otway's *Venice Preserv'd*), wealthy men with or without their wives (the most famous example is Samuel Pepys and his wife Elizabeth), and citizens from the City of London, as well as 'town' people. One commentator lists *'Judges, Wits, Censurers'* in the pit, and in the middle gallery, *'Squires, Beaus, Whores'*, and 'citizens, wives, journey-men, apprentices' – a broad range of social classes.[3]

As in Behn's comedies, discussed in the next section, the 'citizen' present in such an audience might be singled out for satire on the stage, and citizens were consistently the butt of political satire. However, self-styled 'wits' were also satirized. As Samuel Vincent's *Young Gallant's Academy* (1674) indicates, the category of 'gallant' was constantly in danger of sliding into foppishness. Vincent gives mock-instructions on gallant's behaviour at a playhouse: 'having made his honour to the rest of the company, but especially to the vizard-masks [masked women, here assumed to be prostitutes by the would-be gallant] . . . the next step is to give hum to the China orange-wench, and give her her own rate for her oranges... and then to present the fairest to the next vizard-mask'.[4] As this caricature indicates, the dominating presence of 'the gallant' as identified by noticeable codes of behaviour made him a highly visible part of the audience, and invited satire. Other elements of the audience were more enigmatic: while 'vizard-masks' in Vincent's account are prostitutes ('damsels that hunt for prey'), other women, married or 'chaste', might wear vizards in order to attend a play incognito.

Thus the audiences of Restoration London, who interrupted plays and combined to damn them (as happened to Behn's *Lucky Chance*), participated in a sophisticated social exchange whereby the nature of the audience was a constant presence in the comedies which they watched. Aphra Behn's comedies, such as *The Town Fop* and *The Rover*, use masquerade to make reference to the mores of the society before which the plays were performed: a script was a loose framework for an interaction between audience and play.

The dynamic relationship between audience and stage made the theatres a crucible for political and social issues. Prologues and epilogues often made the play's political allegiances plain, or retrospectively turned a particular set of comic events towards contemporary politics; Behn herself seems to have been in trouble over one such epilogue, to *Romulus and Herselia*, in which she attacked the Duke of Monmouth.[5] Moreover, the theatre's reiteration of the quarrels of the Civil War spoke to the continued divisions of that society, and the theatre continued to articulate opposing political views. This is suggested by Behn's repeated satirical conflation of the senex ('old man') figure of the *commedia dell' arte* and the believer in the republican or Cromwellian Good Old Cause of the Civil War.

Cabals of theatregoers sometimes attempted to create a hostile reception for a play even before it was put on. The lobby might take up a political or a moral issue; and Behn's writing drew attacks because of its treatment of issues of gender and morality. In 1686, in her preface to *The Lucky Chance*, she lists the criticism of her play: '[rival poets] when they can no other way prevail with the Town, they charge it with the old never failing Scandal – That 'tis not fit for the Ladys' (Summers, iii. 185). The debate indicates that the presence of women of good reputation in the playhouse audience was a focus for social anxiety. Significantly, the attack on Behn's *The Lucky Chance* illuminates the difficult position of a woman writing in the 'lower' form of comedy, a form used widely by male writers such as Sir Charles Sedley, Sir George Etherege, and especially William Wycherley, whose *The Country Wife* influenced Behn. Behn's own ironic comment on the ethical implications of comic drama – that 'our latter Plays have not done much more towards the amending of men's morals, or their Wit, than hath frequent preaching' ('Epistle to the Reader', *The Dutch Lover*, Summers, i. 222–3) – situates the debate on the morality of comedy in relation to Restoration discourses of moral rectitude generated by religious controversy, and is sceptical of the moral purposes of comedy, seeing comedic discourse as always addressing 'interests'.

As in the sphere of poetry, Behn's position contrasted with that of other women writing in the field. She was economically dependent on the theatre, highly commercial and prolific, and working in sexually and politically charged genres. Katherine Philips, on the other hand, wrote two plays, both translations from Corneille's tragedies: *Pompey* (staged in Dublin, 1663), and *Horace* (staged posthumously in London, 1668). Although both Elizabeth Polwhele and Frances Boothby seem to have written plays during the 1670s, Behn's long career writing for the stage is very different from the production of a few plays.[6] The public nature of her role as a woman writing for a playhouse, for money, and with a political agenda was the aspect of her career which provoked adverse comment and sexual slurs. In response to the playwright Thomas Otway having written a prologue for her, the Whig supporter Thomas Shadwell sneered at *The City Heiress* as '*The City Heresie*'; he attacked its Tory politics, the proliferation of 'women and boys' writing for the playhouse, and Behn herself:

> Poetess *Afra* though she's damned today
> Tomorrow will put up another Play;
> And *Ot[wa]y* must pimp to set her off.[7]

Although Shadwell's attack was political, the reference to pimping was taken up elsewhere. Brown implied that Behn's poet-lovers wrote the plays: 'the least return your admirers could make you for your favours, was first to lend you their assistance, and then oblige with their applause.'[8] The most virulent attack came from Robert Gould in his poem 'The Playhouse. A Satyr'.

29

Gould's sustainedly sexualized attack on Behn as 'Sappho in her wanton fit', ironically calling *The City Heiress* a 'clean piece of wit', is combined with his obsessive return to the prostitutes who frequent the theatre ('Where reeking Punks like Summer Insects swarm') and to the social crisis implied by the fact that not only 'the *Women* in this *Frantick Age*' think they are poets, but also '*Courtier* and *Peasant* equally Possess, I Write'.[9] While Gould's criticism is undoubtedly misogynistic, it cannot be understood, as many critics read it, as simply expressing that contemporary opinion which oppressed women playwrights. The extreme and even pathological nature of Gould's attacks make him something of an unusual case, and we might speculate on their motivation. He began life as a servant; like Behn, he had no classical languages; and like her, he lacked a livelihood. The social fluidity whereby anyone can write and attempt to stage plays is, as he sometimes suggests, that which enables him, like Behn, to intervene in poetic and dramatic discourse. Thus the attacks on Behn, as well as being read as misogynistic, might be seen as responding to and registering anxieties about the social transformations suggested by the changing meanings of the theatre as a cultural institution during the second half of the seventeenth century – a transformation of social, sexual, economic, and political dimensions which marked both the plays produced and the conditions of their production.[10]

It was against this context of an actively politicized audience which paid heightened attention to gender and morality because of the sex of the author, and a highly competitive commercial culture of theatrical production, that Behn's comedies of sexual, political, and financial intrigue were staged. Their engagement with the central preoccupations of her audience – politics, sexuality, finance – meant that they occupied an important position at the intersection of politics and popular culture. Let us now look more closely at these issues at work in Behn's political comedies from the political crises of the 1670s and 1680s.

BEHN'S POLITICAL COMEDIES

[P]ublick Pleasures and Divertisements [are]...the schools of Vertue, where Vice is always either punish'd or disdain'd.

They are secret instructions to the People, in things that 'tis impossible to insinuate into them any other way.

(Summers, iii. 183)

So Behn wrote in the dedication to *The Lucky Chance*. How seriously can such protestations about the reforming role of theatre be taken? Often critics have rather taken Behn at her word, looking into her plays to see what the author thought, or seeing the female leads as representations of Behn's ideals or as mouthpieces for her ideas about the reformation of relations between the sexes. Indeed, criticism of her comedies from Vita Sackville-West to Susan Carlson have seen them in relation to gender ideologies as either 'disappointingly conventional' or suggesting 'qualified . . . rebellion'.[11] Obviously, Behn's comedies address that paper tiger of the Restoration stage, arranged marriage, and they can be read as offering a complex understanding of sexual freedom in and out of marriage. However, as Chapter 2 suggested, it is problematic to read a text as simply expressing the ideas of an author; as was the case in the poetry, we need to see the texts in relation to the contexts that produced them. In this case, we need to take account of the complex signifying system of theatre where many individuals and institutions, as well as writer and audience, have an input into the final product. And as we have seen, theatre was bound up with politics and social issues; any 'secret instructions' that we can find in Behn's plays are likely to involve a complex mixture of politics, economics, and sexuality rather than being simple ethical instructions or straightforward commentaries on the status of women. Therefore, rather than look for 'secret instructions' about Behn's own views on gender, this chapter looks briefly at some of Behn's plays in the context of the sexual, economic, and political patterns they trace, and some of the contradictions they suggest.

Behn had a long and prolific career writing for the theatre: *The Forced Marriage* was produced in 1670, and *The Widow Ranter* was produced at Drury Lane in 1689, after her death; *The Younger Brother* was staged only in 1696. In between came about sixteen other plays – one tragedy, tragicomedies, several sorts of comedy, and possibly several unsigned plays and adaptations.[12] Here I will concentrate on the politicized city comedies of the 1670s and 1680s, focusing on three plays: *Sir Patient Fancy* (produced in the

31

year that the Popish Plot scandal broke, probably staged in January 1678), *The City Heiress* (probably staged in late April 1682), and *The Lucky Chance* (performed in April 1686 by the United Company). *The Rover*, which raises slightly different issues, is dealt with separately in the next section.

As we have seen, theatre held an important place in London social life, and plays both registered and influenced the political ferment and scandals of the period. The influences flowed in both directions, for, as the epilogue to *The Rover II* puts it, the audience 'appear | A Parliament by Play-Bill, summon'd here'. The early years of the Restoration, 1660–7, saw a spate of politicized drama which reworked the questions of the Civil War – who should rule, how social status and wealth should be distributed, what it meant to rule, and what control a ruler might have over religion. Plays such as Sir Robert Howard's *The Committee* (1662), Sir Charles Sedley's *The Mulberry Garden*, and Etherege's *The Comical Revenge* satirized the groups they perceived as having benefited from the Civil War. Such politicization of plays and audiences intensified during the Popish Plot and the Exclusion crisis, terms which refer to a number of political issues from 1678 to the mid-1680s, most importantly the question of whether or not Charles II's brother, the Roman Catholic James, Duke of York, should succeed to the throne. Charles II's death in 1685 was followed by a rebellion by his illegitimate son, James, Duke of Monmouth (this period is the background to Behn's *Love Letters*). Although this rebellion was quelled, James II did fly the country in 1688. As was suggested in the Introduction, the terms Whig and Tory began to be used in the period 1670–88 to describe supporters of religious dissent and political radicalism of various kinds. Tories, whether Roman Catholic or not themselves, were prepared to support the succession of James II. Whigs and supporters of the Good Old Cause regarded themselves as 'united in their dislike of arbitrary government, Roman Catholicism, prelacy, and the persecution of Protestants'.[13] All this affected debate in the theatre, amongst plays and audiences. Behn herself wrote in the cause of Charles II. So, like tendentious jokes, her political comedies might well have met with audiences unsympathetic to her view; and those audiences were likely to be sitting very close to the forestage that extended into the theatre. They were expected to talk back.

The controversy of this period – especially 1678 to 1682 –

produced a range of political plays, of which the most famous is probably Otway's *Venice Preserv'd*. Audiences flocked to the flood of political drama in 1680–2, and the first three years of the 1680s saw the production of twelve new plays a year (by contrast, the next six years produced only four each). The closure of the King's Company in 1682 changed the situation, and when the theatres revived after the so-called Glorious Revolution of 1688 – in which the Protestants William and Mary replaced James II as rulers – plays and tastes had changed substantially.

Soon after she began writing for the stage, therefore, Behn's plays became enmeshed in social and political controversy: in 1687 an epilogue written for one of her plays claims 'Long have we turn'd the point of our just Rage, | On the half Wits and Critics of the Age.' Controversy was the norm, and, like other plays of the period, Behn's comedies put theatre at the centre of political dispute. That the stage and audience were exuberantly aware of politics is indicated by the fact that even at the end of the 1680s a play had to be stopped 'less the two parties made violence one upon another'.[14] In this context comedy was both an intimate and a polemical medium.

The emergence of such political positions and language influenced the kinds of comedies Behn wrote in important ways. This becomes clear if we compare *The Town Fop, or Sir Timothy Tawdry* (1676), one of Behn's early comedies, with her later political comedies. Addressing English social mores, this early play stages the undoing of a legal marriage – a marriage bound up with financial arrangements – and dramatizes the rejection of a moneyed lover of 'improper' social values. Bellmour has vowed to marry Celinda but gives into economic pressure from his uncle Plotwell to marry Diana, who loves him. Eventually Diana, recognizing that Bellmour can never love her, begs Plotwell to 'undo that Knot, that ties us two', and the marriage is dissolved in favour of the earlier exchange of vows between Bellmour and Celinda.

The play is built from the familar scenes of Restoration comedy: a discovery in a bedchamber, a masquerade, a cross-dressed courtship where Diana falls for a disguised Clarinda. It uses these building blocks to reorganize as comedy an earlier topical and potentially tragic play, George Wilkins's *The Miseries of Enforced Marriage* (1607): the 'happy ending' turns on Bellmour and Diana being allowed to divorce. Thus, Behn's comedies are already addressing the main issues of Restoration comedy and suggesting new ethical solutions to unhappy marriages similar to that proposed in Wycherley's *The Country Wife*. Very rapidly these ethical questions became tightly bound to politics; and the audience's experience of her plays becomes an increasingly complex web of fascination, disgust, and sympathy.

From the beginning of the Popish Plot crisis, Behn's plays use inappropriate marriages to dramatize social antagonisms between what the play represents as 'citizens' (coded politically as wealthy republicans or supporters of Cromwell) and the young 'royalists'. It is at this point that the plays begin to focus on the Whigs as the fascinating enemy, and to blend sexual intrigue and politics. They repeatedly return to the question of the Good Old Cause (religious dissent, republicanism, rebellion), as Behn's plays make Cromwellians the objects of prolonged satire and invite the audience to enjoy their punishment. Moreover, the reader can trace in the later plays a tension between the repeated repudiation of and the continuing focus upon republican politics.

Following *The Town Fop*, the comedy *Sir Patient Fancy* sets political and sexual questions against each other. This play was staged by January 1678 and fuses comic and political discourse. The question of arranged marriages, made on 'the formal recommendations of a Parent' (Summers, iv. I. i) and the discontents of a woman married to an Old Causer are explored. It reworks sections of Molière's play *La Malade imaginaire* (particularly the figure of Argan), situating them in the London cultures of well-off Puritan and Presbyterian merchants and impoverished gallants. So the plot turns on the deceit of sexually and politically nasty old men by witty, beautiful, and royalist women, to the great economic advantage of their royalist lovers. The play opens with Sir Patient's fashionable young wife bewailing her fate:

> LADY FANCY. . . . set up with an old formal doting sick Husband, and a Herd of snivelling grinning Hypocrites, that call themselves the teaching Saints; who under pretence of securing me to the number of their Flock, do sneer upon me, pat my Breasts, and cry fie, fie upon this fashion of tempting Nakedness.
>
> (Summers, iv. II. i. 26–7)

Lady Fancy mimics the sanctimonious voices of the 'snivelling

...Hypocrites'; and she, and the play, take their hypocritical politics and religion as licence for her attempts to escape.

For example, she is interrupted entertaining her lover Wittmore in the garden. He pretends to her husband, the hypochondriac 'citizen' Sir Patient, that he is one 'Fainlove', whose father Patient apparently knew in their mutual heyday under Cromwell:

> SIR PAT. What, not *Mr Fainlove*'s Son of *Yorkshire*, who was knighted in the good days of the late Lord Protector?
>
> > [*Takes off his hat*
>
> WIT. The same Sir, I am in, but how to come off again the Devil take me if I know.
>
> SIR PAT. He was...a good Commonwealthsman...ah, Mr *Fainlove*, he and I have seen better days, and wish we cou'd have foreseen these that have arriv'd.
>
> > (Summers, iv. II. i. 30)

The several puns on the assumed name 'Fainlove' emphasize the interconnection of politics (the feigned love of republican politics by Wittmore) and desire (fain love – his desire for Lady Fancy). Sir Patient is deceived into thinking that 'Fainlove' courts his daughter rather than his wife. He then readily substantiates his own deception by providing Wittmore/Fainlove with the kind of pedigree he would wish in a son-in-law – the rich son of an ex-Commonwealthsman, prudent, unencumbered, and educated in Geneva, home of Puritanism and implying religious dissent and dislike of arbitrary rule.[15]

Notably, when *Sir Patient Fancy* came on the stage, the main concern of the public was not with the danger posed by nonconformists like Sir Patient. The informer Titus Oates had just disclosed to Charles II details of the so-called Popish Plot. By November, when the play was staged, the crisis was public and, as Roger North later put it, 'it was not safe for anyone to show scepticism' about the idea that a large number of Catholics were plotting the downfall of the King.[16] Apparently flowing counter to public opinion, the play counterposes gallants and nonconformists, proposing dissenters rather than Catholics as a social and political problem.

In presenting Sir Patient as 'cautiously rich' and 'vainly proud...of his rebellious opinion' (Summers, iv. II. i. 26), the play satirizes values directly pertinent to the political conflicts of London in and after the Civil War, indicating that past and present political differences are accompanied by significant differences of culture. The past invoked by Sir Patient – the 'better days' of the Commonwealth – is represented as leading to a present in which Sir Patient Fancy (like Sir Feeble Fainwoud and Sir Cautious Fulbank in *The Lucky Chance*) is able to control a household and buy a young wife because of his capital. This capital, the play suggests, was ill-gotten during the Civil War, and we once again encounter Behn's tendency to link 'genuine' nobility to appropriate fortune in the way Sir Patient is presented as socially insufficient to the power money confers on him.

While Old Cromwellians like Sir Patient prosper, the next generation of aristocrats – whose families were impoverished by the war – are plotting, using skill, intelligence, and natural attractions under the restored Stuart regime to regain social control. In *Sir Patient Fancy*, set after the Restoration of Charles II, the young royalist gallants are swimming with the political tide of monarchy that the City men are represented as resisting. As the play progresses, the gallants and women locked into unwanted marriages gain sexual and then economic and social primacy. Royalist gallants and women are rewarded in the closing scenes and a dramatic conversion is teased out: Sir Patient is won away from parsimonious hypochondria and the Good Old Cause to gallantry. Lady Fancy, far from being a reformed wife, continues as the lover of the young royalist.

This denouement is achieved when the Sir Patient's nephew and heir, Leander, persuades his uncle to fool his wife into betraying her affair with Wittmore by the carnivalesque device of playing dead (which can be compared with the pre-Civil-War *The Knight of the Burning Pestle*). As he lies in his coffin, Lady Fancy refers to 'the stinking Corps of my quondam Cuckold' (Summers, iv. v. i. 112), and Sir Patient realizes that he has doted on an adulteress. His recognition of his wife's deceit leads to the establishment – or, as the lovers regard it, the re-establishment – of Lady Fancy's earlier relationship with Wittmore. Love and money seem to be able to make a new social order. Indeed, the ending of the play partially recapitulates the ending of *The Town Fop* in the presentation of an economically secure separation: during his doting phase Sir Patient has settled £8,000 on Lady Fancy. As in *The Town Fop*, the audience is invited to condone a compromise. But a significant difference is that in *Sir Patient Fancy* the economic and sexual conflicts are politically overdetermined – they show the favoured figures triumphing, and those figures are all royalist, or, as they would probably have been read by contemporaries, supporters of Charles II and his brother James.

Indeed, while Sir Patient's coffin-scene 'resurrection' leads to the establishment of Lady Fancy's freedom, it also leads to his own social and political rebirth:

LADY FANCY. My Husband! – I'm betray'd –

SIR PAT. Husband! I do defy thee, Satan, thou greater Whore than she of *Babylon*; thou Shame, thou Abomination to thy Sex.

LADY FANCY. Rail on, whilst I dispose myself to laugh at thee.

SIR PAT. *Leander*, call all the House in to be a Witness of our Divorce.

[*Exit Leander*

LADY FANCY. Do, and all the World, and let 'em know the Reason.

SIR PAT. Methinks I find an Inclination to swear, – to curse my self and thee, that I cou'd no better discern thee; nay, I'm so chang'd from what I was, that I think I cou'd even approve of Monarchy and Church-Discipline, I'm so truly convinc'd I have been a Beast and an Ass.

(Summers, iv. v. i. 113).

There is no doubt that the joke is on Sir Patient. Lady Fancy laughs in his face, and Wittmore explains that they 'have long been Lovers, but want of Fortune' (Summers, iv. v. i.) made them contrive the marriage to the alderman. Sir Patient is 'reformed'; but unlike the reformations of other Restoration comedies, in which rakes and libertines turn to the straight and narrow path of marital monogamy, this reformation sees Sir Patient turning *to* the libertine life-style. His use of words like 'convinc'd', more usually associated with conversion *to* religious dissent, reinforces the paradoxical nature of this particular change. When he turns to the audience to suggest that we take 'example by my Reformation' (Summers, iv. v. i. 115) he uses language saturated with implications of the Puritan reformation of manners to describe its opposite, his embracing of a life of sexual liberty. It is, also, a political conversion which saves for the right political side a figure who has given the audience comic pleasure. Sir Patient ends by saying 'I ... will turn Spark, they live the merriest Lives – keep some City Mistress, go to Court, and hate all Conventicles' (Summers, iv. v. i. 115).

However, Behn's later plays abandon this strategy of closing on

37

the incorporation of the comic outsider into what the play presents as the proper social ethos when the political debate polarized; as Charles II aged, it became ever clearer that his death would cause a problem of succession and, accordingly, the debate in the press and in theatres became fiercer.

In *Sir Patient Fancy* the potential for change in society, in favour of Tory/monarchist groups, is articulated by the caricaturing of the sexual desires and foolishness of the post-Civil-War City merchants, vulnerable to the landless but witty new male gallants through the medium of women. Women function both as sexual property and active agents, though not usually acting in consort. As Wittmore puts it, 'Many a wealthy Citizen, sir, has contributed to the maintenance of a younger Brother's Mistress' (Summers, iv. v. i. 114). Women, like Lady Fancy and the female leads of Behn's later plays *The City Heiress* and *The Lucky Chance*, become social, political, and economic double agents, who through their many-layered intercourse with both the nonconformist alderman and the aristocratic gallants are able to make their sexual activities profitable and secure their own situation. Moreover, they are able to use sexual allegiance to redirect other resources which the City men are seen as having amassed during and after the Civil War. The beneficiaries of such redirection are, of course, the gallants. In Behn's political comedies women are seen dismantling from within the sexually and politically oppressive institutions coded as belonging to the past (and summed up as marriage to aged ex-Cromwellian City men), and turning economic and sexual resources towards a distant, but potentially achievable future of intertwined sexual and political liberty.

The comic working-out of an alliance of sexual, economic, and political productivity at the expense of socially, politically, and sexually unsuitable radicals is reworked in *The Roundheads: or, The Good Old Cause* (1681), staged at the height of political turmoil. This actually adapts a play published and performed in the last moments of the Interregnum, John Tatham's *The Rump* (published in 1659 and 1660). With an eye to the market for political scandal, Behn reworks history to produce two pairs of lovers caught up in a political crisis ostensibly of 1659 – the moment of Charles II's Restoration – but with the vocabulary of 1681.[17] Contemporary accounts of this moment suggested that 'the humour of the city [was] the same as it was forty years ago' – it looked 'as if London will set up for a Commonwealth' (i.e. republic).[18] The deepening crisis is suggested by comparing the endings of *Sir Patient Fancy* and *The Roundheads*: where *Sir Patient Fancy* ends with the conversion of a republican to royalism, the similar conversion of Lady Lambert in *The Roundheads* is very clearly set against the harsh and permanent punishment of all the rest of the Rump and its factions.

By the next year, 1682, Charles II had to some extent pushed underground the diverse opposition groups, and it was after the dispersion of the Whig radicals that *The City Heiress* was staged. If, as Behn suggested in the dedication to *The Lucky Chance*, plays offer 'secret instructions to the People', then the instructions, or ethical messages, offered in *The City Heiress* are complex to the point of confusion. It seems to be a sharp satire of the very audience sitting so close to the stage, and of their flawed social and political community. Thus, where *Sir Patient Fancy* offered the gallants as a point of identification, this complex political comedy both invites the audience to empathize with the central male figure and signals his sexual, ethical, and economic unreliability. Another factor hindering the audience from establishing any straightforward political or ethical position is the fact that in this play the aged republican and the royalist gallant are inextricably interwoven through their sexual relations with one woman. The fascination which the spectacle of republicanism, seen as an object of terror, held for contemporary audiences is here even more clearly visible than in Behn's earlier plays, and this comedy provides a complex and ambivalent account of sexual, political, and economic relations. However, while its close relationship to political issues is sometimes said to render the play unstageable for modern audiences, these complexities are bound up with comedy and sexual satire which would make it a pleasurable theatrical experience.

At the play's opening Wilding, a nephew-gallant, is faced with disinheritance on the grounds of debauchery. He denounces his uncle's excesses and politicized feats which combine consumption and corruption:

> WILDING. ...amongst the lusty-stomacht Whigs that daily nose your publik Dinners, some may be found, that either for Money, Charity, or Gratitude, may requite your Treats. You keep open House to all the Party, not for Mirth, Generosity or good Nature, but for Roguery. You

cram the Brethren, the pious City-Gluttons, with Good Cheer, Good
Wine, and Rebellion in abundance, gormandizing all Comers and
Goers, of all Sexes, Sorts, Opinions and Religions...and all in hopes
of debauching the King's Liege-people into Commonwealths; and
rather than lose a Convert, you'll pimp for him. These are your nightly
Debauches.

(Summers, ii. I. i. 207–8)

Where Wilmore in *The Rover* is promiscuous, Wilding is described
by his whore, Diana, as 'a Wit with a Pox' (Summers, i. II. ii. 229);
the syphilis is an indication that his behaviour does have
consequences. And Diana's understanding of him is reinforced
by comments from other figures, including Sir Timothy Treat-All.
Thus, the play has as its central figure a man who, on the one hand,
(with the audience's invited endorsement) denounces his uncle's
hypocritical political debauchery and, on the other, courts two
women, Charlot (a virgin heiress) and Lady Galliard (a rich widow,
first played by Elizabeth Barry), while also keeping a whore. His
status as a syphilitic must qualify the audience's immediate or
conclusive identification of him as a 'hero'. Rather, he and 'his' pox
can be read as a particularly vivid figure for the circulation of
money and sex, in that a sexual transaction with Wilding is likely to
leave the partner marked by illness. As suggested earlier, the
gallant does not represent a stable positive value or idea; in this
case Wilding's syphilis stands as a perverse index of social ties and
connections in a society which this play presents as simultaneously
bound tightly together and deeply fractured. Indeed, the high cost
of Wilding's (useless) medical bill even figures as the ultimate
reason that his uncle casts him out:

SIR TIMOTHY. No...you have talkt me out of many a fair Thousand;
have had ye out of all the Bayliffs, Serjeants, and Constables
Clutches about Town, Sir; have bought you out of all the Surgeons,
Apothecaries and pocky Doctors Hands, that ever pretended to
cure incurable Diseases.

(Summers, ii. I. i. 204)

Sir Timothy, the old Commonwealthsman, has been paying for
Wilding's syphilis to be treated. In response, Wilding accuses his
uncle of buying goods for consumption by 'all Sexes, Sorts,
Opinions' – food, wine, sex used as bribes for the Good Old,
Cromwellian cause.

Yet Wilding himself is locked into a similar circuit. Although his situation is superficially different in that it is driven by desire and financial needs rather than political ends, it repeats the interlocking economy of sex, finance, and politics. Once he has been cast out by his uncle for his political sympathies he needs money to support his desires, and courts both a widow, 'young, rich, and beautiful', and 'a rich City-Heiress' (Summers, ii. I. i. 209). Economic vulnerability recasts his demands for sexual favours into *offers* of sexual courtship for which he might reap financial reward. Actions such as giving his whore, Diana, a ring which Charlot gave him as a love token make him as much a kept gallant as a hero. As Diana explains, she is unpaid; but Wilding tries to retain her, she says, 'with hopes of a rich Wife, whose fortune I am to lavish' (Summers, ii, II. ii. 228).

Despite his own deeply compromised position, driven by economic necessity to live off women, Wilding argues for a libertine ethics of love whereby women are morally wrong if they sleep with men for financial gain:

> WILDING. According to the strictest Rules of Honour,
> Beauty should still be the Reward of Love,
> Not the vile Merchandize of Fortune,
>
> . . . . .
>
> She's only infamous, who to her Bed
> For Interest takes some nauseous Clown she hates:
> And though a Jointure or a Vow in publick
> Be her Price, that makes her but the dearer Whore.
>
> (Summers, ii. IV. i. 264)

Any audience, Restoration or modern, is forced to respond in a complicated way to the play because of the paradoxical nature of this central figure and by the complexities he sets in motion. For example, although the play ends with the marriage of Diana – the ironically named whore – any satisfying closure on economic equilibrium is undermined by her comments on the price she pays for economic security. Paired with Wilding's uncle, a man whose political activities the play presents as reprehensible, Diana vividly articulates the implications of sacrifice to economic necessity. Betty speaks literally of Diana 'keeping' Wilding:

> BETTY. I verily believe the way to keep your young Lover, is to marry this old one: for what Youth and Beauty cannot purchase, Money and Quality may.

41

DIANA. Ay, but to be oblig'd to lie with such a Beast; ay, there's the
Devil, Betty. Ah, when I find the difference of their Embraces.

The soft dear arms of Wilding round my Neck.
From those cold feeble ones of this Dotard.

(Summers, ii. v. iii. 286)

When Sir Timothy arrives, the next inevitable step is made clear in
her aside: 'If I must marry him, give him Patience to endure the
Cuckolding, good Heaven' (v. iii), and the solution Wilding forces
Diana to adopt inevitably undercuts his own libertine rhetoric.
The emphatic characterization of Wilding as a poxed and dubious
libertine means that the triumph of money and politics is qualified
by continuing marital and sexual discontent. So the 'secret
instructions' the audience might receive are far from obvious.

Although it ends in the multiple marriages characteristic of
comedy, the play can be read as questioning marital contracts.
Diana, although she engineers economic security, is also traded
between nephew and uncle as 'used goods', and Wilding arranges
that she will be the vehicle of his revenge by being used in a quasi-
incestuous sexual humiliation for his uncle. This ensures that she is
sexually shared between men of different generations in practically
a father–son relation. Thus, the conflict of political values between
generations suggested in *Sir Patient Fancy* is even more troubled in
The City Heiress. The competition for women between the royalist
gallant and the nonconformist old man is situated within an only
slightly adapted version of an incestuous family romance where
uncle and nephew are substituted for father and son. Indeed, like a
father, Sir Timothy weeps as he bewails the youth who 'before he
fell to Toryism' was 'a sober, Civil Youth ... and then I had Hopes
of him' (Summers, ii. I. i. 205).

The audience is not offered any clear or obvious way to place
Wilding's sexual mores in relation to his politics. The syphilitic
philanderer is not fully a hero on the sexual front nor completely
compromised politically; it is an index of the complexity of the
play that, in a comedy in which other politico-sexual wrongdoers
are violently punished, Wilding remains as hero himself riven
with contradictions and bound in – even at the fractured centre of
– the flawed and exploitative society he inhabits.

While the audience is offered an ambivalent and qualified
triumph of an altogether worldly and disappointed royalism, the
play stages the defeat of republicanism in the person of the uncle

Treat-All and his lover Sensure by inviting the audience to enjoy prolonged scenes of comic violence and political and sexual humiliation. Although morally dubious, Wilding's political and economic triumph contrasts sharply with Treat-All's multiple degradation, effected both through his final entrapment into marriage with Diana and when his nephew fools him into accepting the crown of Poland (a Catholic elective monarchy).

Theatrically, Treat-All is spectacularly humiliated (in an incident taken from Thomas Middleton's *Mad World My Masters*) when Wilding disguises himself as a burglar. Surprised in the middle of night, bound and robbed, he vents his anger: 'These are your Tory Rogues,' he cries, 'but we shall cry quits with you, Rascals, ere long; and it we do come to our Old Trade of Plunder and Sequestration, we shall so handle ye – we'll spare neither Prince, Peer, nor Prelate' (Summers, ii. 282–3). Thus, at the moment of his greatest humiliation, Treat-All's political ambitions are exposed as purely envious; he wants to return to the time of the Civil War only so that he, not they, shall be strongest in crime. So, the victim of the scene is determined as undeserving of sympathy for the audience. The criminal self-disclosure which the play puts into his mouth legitimates him as a proper target for comic violence.

His threats are ineffectual – Sir Timothy is comprehensively defeated, trussed up like turkey, and physically as well as politically immobilized. But the ultimate sign of his reprehensible conduct is provided by a linking of sexual and political hypocrisy in a scene showing the violent physical humiliation of the punningly named 'Sensure', his mistress, who flees from his bed during the disguised Wilding's midnight raid. This scene is of the sort frequently found in anti-Puritan prose satire, where Puritan men and women are exposed at their lascivious pranks. But Behn theatricalizes a familiar scene with a particular violence, a politicized aggression which we might relate to the crisis of 1681–2. Sensure accidentally puts on the alderman's gown as she tries to escape from the old man's bed, and the audience is invited to enjoy the spectacle of her violent punishment, licensed as it is because she stands for so many anti-Tory and anti-social crimes:

> DRESSWELL. The sanctify'd Jilt professes Innocence, yet has the Badge of her Occupation about her Neck.   [*Pulls off the Coat*
> SENSURE. Ah, Misfortune, I have mistook his Worship's Coat for my Gown.   [*A little Book drops out of her Bosom*

43

DRESSWELL. ... Here, gag, and bind her.   [*Exit Dress.*
SENSURE. Hold, hold, I am with Child!
LABOIR. Then you'll go near to miscarry a Babe of Grace.

(Summers, ii. v. i. 279)

Sensure is a sexual threat (a mother of bastards), a hypocrite (a Puritan mistress), and takes unlawful authority upon herself (she is caught in an alderman's gown). Her religion is exposed as a matter of pretence; her violent degradation goes far beyond that of Sir Timothy. Her accidental wearing of the alderman's gown of office ridicules the office itself, associating it with femininity and hypocrisy as it covers the body of an unchaste woman; and we witness the officially comic scene of her being bound, gagged, and mocked by Dresswell's agent, Laboir. Laboir puns on her 'miscarrying' the enlightenment promised by nonconformist religion; and her manhandling and punishment by Dresswell and Laboir contrast with the play's treatment of the whore, Diana, who, despite being sexually experienced, engineers an undesirable but materially comfortable match with Sir Timothy. The crucial distinction determining the punishments of Diana and Sensure is in the political complexion of the man each slept with. In its contrasting treatment of two 'unchaste' women, one of whom suffers physical violence, the play reaches an extreme of comic violence against the Whigs.

Sensure is punished, Diana is discontented, Wilding is poxed. Is this comedy? If we answer yes, we must acknowledge that such comedy incorporates large elements of violence and invites the audience to take pleasure in punishment, a pleasure which continues to the end of the play, where we find that Wilding has triumphed completely over his uncle:

WILDING. I'll propose fairly now; if you'll be generous and pardon all,
    I'll render your Estate back during Life...
    I have a Fortune here that will maintain me,
    Without even wishing for your Death.

(Summers, ii. v. v. 298)

Wilding is in a position to restore his uncle's 'Estate' to him for his lifetime, provided that he supports 'the rights of just Succession'. Only once the wealth and power have been redistributed is some negotiation possible between the men. This triumph of Tory youth (albeit compromised) over aged, lascivious Whig merchants is offered to the audience as comic closure; the compromises of *Sir Patient Fancy* have quite disappeared.

The City Heiress confirms and extends the pattern of Behn's plays in which sexuality, finance, and politics are interconnected, and in which women redirect their sexual and economic favours from sexually and politically nasty old men to royalist gallants like Wilding. It also, however, indicates the escalating violence with which the Good Old Cause of republicanism and religious dissent is treated in Behn's plays of this period, which increasingly invite the audience to take pleasure in the staged defeat of republicanism. The linking of sexual punishment to politics indicates the powerful frisson in which the Good Old Cause, a cause simultaneously fascinating and repellent, held for contemporaries.

What roles, then, are played by the old republican criminals the Old Causers, which these plays satirize? And what relation do they bear to other characteristics of the Restoration stage?

Behn's next urban comedy, *The Lucky Chance*, was produced in the year after Charles II's death and the defeat of Monmouth's rebellion at Sedgemoor. James II had come to the throne, apparently for good. Once again, this play takes City aldermen as the objects of its satire; and it channels economic, sexual, and political benefits once more, through sexual intrigue, to the gallants. Throughout the play sex is exchanged for money, mapping the politics of both young and old through the theatrical mechanism of discovery. Fidelis Morgan, commenting that the 'obvious glory of the play is its disgusting old men', points to the play's fascinated concentration on what it presents as the physiological, moral, and above all political bankruptcy of two old Cromwellian aldermen in the City of London, Sir Feeble Fainwoud and Sir Cautious Fulbank.[19] Sir Feeble is about to be married to Leticia, who has been forced to abandon her gallant, Bellmour; Sir Cautious is already married to Julia, beloved of Gayman. The plot traces the reuniting of the pairs of lovers, despite the marriages of the women. Once again, the earlier contracts are given primacy; as Leticia puts it, ''Tis not a Marriage, since my Bellmour lives; I The Consummation were Adultery' (Summers, ii. II. 217). On the way Sir Cautious is exposed as willing to sacrifice his wife's virtue in order to escape payment of gambling debts, illuminating both his failure to understand aristocratic codes of honour and his willingness to see his wife as sexual capital. He agrees to lend her to Gayman, 'A single Night – to have – to hold – possess – and so forth, at discretion' (ii. IV. i. 255).

The play's climax is organized in a sequence of bedroom scenes which brilliantly exploit both the proximity of the Restoration stage to the audience and the distance of its framing, like a picture or peep-show, within the proscenium arch. Such a stage offered discoveries of areas further back into it as painted scenes slid away; and, as Peter Holland argues, these were mainly used in tragedy – except by Behn, who, as here, uses them repeatedly for comic revelations. As Elin Diamond has pointed out, such discoveries framed and specularized the body of the actress; however, in Behn's political comedies they also serve to suggest and expose the labyrinthine plotting of the characters.

In this sequence of bedroom scenes the audience watches the action move backwards and forwards on the stage, shifting from garden to chamber, to antechamber, to bedroom and back. Claiming sex with Julia (Lady Fulbank) as payment for gambling debts, her old lover, Gayman, is brought to Sir Cautious in a chest:

> SIR CAUTIOUS. (*Lifting up the Chest-lid*). So, you are come, I see – (*Goes, and locks the door*)
>
> . . .
>
> *Sir Cautious peeps into the Bed-chamber*
> LADY FULBANK. (*within*). Come, Sir Cautious, I shall fall asleep, and then you'll waken me.
> SIR CAUTIOUS. Ay, my dear, I'm coming – she's in Bed – I'll go put out the Candle, and then –
> GAYMAN. Ay, I'll warrant you for my part –
>
> (Summers, ii. V. iv. 269)

Carefully orchestrated stage business sets up the scene; and the audience becomes aware that Sir Cautious is morally reprehensible through the action which takes place between inner and outer stage, beginning with Sir Cautious welcoming the trunk in the garden and retreating, as the moment of multiple disclosure comes closer, towards the framed, inner playing spaces, ending up with the substitution of Gayman for Cautious in the bedroom.

This process of discovering also shows the superior forces gradually gaining control of the plot – as when Gayman is able to use the morally reprehensible Cautious to find a way to Julia.[20] The bedroom scene is followed by one in the 'Anti-chamber', in which Sir Cautious spies on and overhears the lovers:

LADY FULBANK. Oh! You unkind – what have you made me do? Unhand
me, false Deceiver – let me loose –
SIR CAUTIOUS. Made her do? – so, so – 'tis done – I'm glad of that –
[*Aside peeping*
(Summers, ii. v. v. 217)

Thus suspense is generated by shifts of scene, together with the
spectacle of Lady Fulbank's body. These emphasize Lady Fulbank
and Gayman as the empathetic centre of the scene, with Sir
Cautious a marginalized, impotent voyeur of his own cuckoldry;
and the disclosure of his willingness to sell his wife's chastity
coincides with the re-establishment of primary relations and
permits his theatrical exclusion from both centre stage and role as
husband.

Throughout the play the sexual and domestic stand as a figure
for the political. A case in point is the impotence of Sir Feeble: 'a
jolly old fellow, whose activity has all got into his tongue, a very
excellent teaser, but neither youth nor beauty can grind his
dudgeon to an edge' (Summers, ii. I. i. 215). Part of the
'disgusting' quality which Morgan finds in the figures of the
two old men is foregrounded for the audience by Sir Feeble's
adoption of baby talk. While he anticipates the joys of his
wedding night in nursery babble, Leticia weeps with disgust:

SIR FEEBLE. He, ods bobs, we'll do't, sweetheart, her's to 't. [*Drinks again*
LETICIA. I die but to imagine it, wou'd I were dead indeed –
SIR FEEBLE. Ha-hum – how's this? Tears upon the wedding day? Why,
why – you baggage you, ye little Ting, Fool's face, away you Rogue,
you're naughty, you're naughty. (*Patting and playing and following
her*) Look – look – look now, buss it – buss it – buss it and friends;
did'ums beat its none silly baby, away you little Hussey, away and
pledge me.

(Summers, ii. I. iii. 204)

The old man, a second time a child, treats his young wife like a
baby to be cajoled and mumbled. As Behn suggested in her
preface (see the conclusion to this chapter, p. 59), sex scenes have
meaning in relation to the overall plotting of the play: in this
comedy, such sexual 'disgustingness' points directly towards
political disgustingness. The play's extended concentration on
loathsome old men repeats Behn's earlier invitations to be
fascinated and disgusted by the porno-political habits of the old

Civil War revolutionaires.

The Lucky Chance was performed in the aftermath of the juridicial punishment of those who had supported the Duke of Monmouth in his attempt to gain the throne. The failure of his rebellion had spawned punitive trails in which some men were convicted on the evidence of one of the rebels, Lord Grey of Werke (on whom Philander in Behn's *Love Letters* is based), who had turned state's evidence. Prisoners from the rebellion were kept in terrible conditions; the state tried 1,300 men, of whom 250 were executed (a process which depended on two independent witnesses coming forward), 850 were transported, and 200 died in prison or were pardoned. The Quaker John Whiting commented on the executions:

> Forcing poor Men to hale about Mens Quarters, like Horse-Flesh, or Carrion, to boil and hang them up as Monuments of their Cruelty and Inhumanity for the Terror of others...lost King *James* the Hearts of many.[21]

It is against such a background of apparently complete and violent defeat of the Whigs that we can judge Behn's brilliant comic staging in this play. One might see her toothless, senile, impotent radicals as registering the apparent defeat of the Whig cause. Certainly, their helplessness distinguishes them from the more energetic Old Causers, such as Sir Patient Fancy – who only *thought* he was ill – and the very active Sir Timothy Treat-All in *The City Heiress*. *The Lucky Chance* gave an extra twist to the attack on Whiggism, whose apparent defeat made it available for triumphalist satire.

Behn's concern in her drama with republican figures suggests the lingering fascination with objects of disgust shared between plays and audiences. This dynamic is central to the plays: the sexual transgressions of aged republicans (presented at length and in riveting comic detail) stand for and reinforce the scandalous nature of anti-government political opinions. The oscillation between fascination and disgust with Whiggery is the mainspring of Behn's political plays from the years of the Exclusion crisis and after. And in *The Lucky Chance* it would appear that the fascination exerted by Whigs was no less when they seemed to be defeated, and thus available for representation as mumbling fools, aged, senile, and ultimately foredone by their own cupidity. The triumph of the moment appears to endorse the power of Behn's attack.

The sexual ethics and possible resolutions of dreadful marriages also become more complicated, with *The Lucky Chance* offering a fairly full examination of one woman's compromise in Julia's (Lady Fulbank's) discovery that her husband is willing to prostitute her for money. When she works out what we, the audience, have already seen in the discovery scenes – that Sir Cautious planned for Gayman to come to her bed – she responds:

> LADY FULBANK. I am convinc'd the fault was all my Husband's – And here I vow, – by all things just and sacred, To separate for ever from his Bed. *(Kneels)*
>
> (Summers, ii. v. vii. 273)

Accordingly, the play ends with Sir Cautious telling Gayman, 'I bequeath my Lady to you – with my Whole Estate' (v. vii). So, in gaining a compromised measure of sexual freedom, Lady Fulbank also gains, at least for the future, economic security for herself and her Tory gallant.

Behn's career in dramatic comedy ended with her plays echoing the dominant position of James II's government, worked out in terms of economics, sexuality, and politics, and using the theatrical metaphor of discovery. However, the situation changed again, and James was defeated. Behn's posthumously performed and undated play *The Widow Ranter* was performed under the new regime of William and Mary. Thus throughout her theatrical career and after her death, whether or not Behn's plays offer secret instructions to the audience, their comic plots are tightly bound to the social and political lives of their audiences. And in plays like *The Lucky Chance* and *Sir Patient Fancy* the political aspects of the play are interwoven with a highly self-conscious use of the potential of the Restoration stage, discussed in the next section, on *The Rover*.

THE ROVER: THE SIGNS OF CARNIVAL

The Rover, or the Banish'd Cavaliers (1677), probably Behn's best-known play, set in Naples during carnival, takes up similar political issues to the comedies set in London. However, instead of posing them as an antithesis between ancient, quasi-republican aldermen and suffering young gallants, it follows the fortunes of a set of royalists adrift in Europe during the Protectorate of Oliver Cromwell, and returns, yet again, to the political issues of the Civil War, raising the familiar issues of economic, sexual, and political change. Distinctively, this play emphasizes the readability and unreadability of signs such as dress, name, or location. It takes a carnival setting, which is crucial to the plot, allowing three sisters to marry three gallants. However, any understanding of carnival as liberating is qualified by the fate of the courtesan Angelica Bianca and by the emphasis on its sinister qualities.

The play takes its cue from Thomas Killigrew's ten-act play, *Thomaso*, written and set in the 1650s. Killigrew dramatizes the life of exiled or migrant supporters of Charles Stuart; *The Rover* takes up one incident from Killigrew's long text to make a comedy set around the affective and economic relations between the sexes. It reworks the events of Cromwell's Protectorship in relation to the emerging politics of dissent in Charles II's reign and at the moment of the play's first production at the Duke's House, Dorset Gardens. Like *The Roundheads*, it reshapes a play from the Civil War period; but unlike Behn's comedies of the later 1670s and 1680s it is set outside England at a moment of dangerous but exciting fluidity. It also differs from the comedies set in post-Civil-War London in that it posits marriage and economic stability as a possible – though not likely – outcome of the wartime romances.

The Rover's epilogue draws out a political implication from the 'cavalier' figures of Willmore, Belville, Frederick, with the ironic suggestion that:

> The banisht Cavaliers! A Roving Blade!
> A popish Carnival! a Masquerade!
> The Devil's in 't if this will please the nation,
> In these our blessed Times of Reformation,
> When Conventicling is so much in Fashion.
>
> (Epilogue, Summers, i. 105)

This makes clear that the play reworks the political past in relation to the present, and also calls attention to the play's relationship with the audience, who may approve or disapprove, but may also act as interpreters, readers of the signs of the plot. Not only the epilogue but the play as a whole foreground the presence of the audience, challenging it to follow the clues and read the enigmatic signs of masks, theatre, and disguise. The setting in carnival time reflects the presence of vizards and other disguises both in the audience and on stage, figuring disguise and masquerade as, in Terry Castle's words, 'a highly visible public institution and a highly charged image...a modern emblem, carrying multiple, indeed protean, metaphoric possibilities'.[22] Disguise requires both characters and audience to have a particularly expert eye in order to differentiate virgins from prostitutes and financial opportunities from trickery – with a further twist added by the fact that actresses were perceived as supplementing their income by working as prostitutes.

The London theatre of the 1670s does seem to have been an accepted place of disguise, hiding, and assignation. But carnival, in its relation to the Roman Catholic church year, involved the momentary suspension of hierarchy and the taking on of rituals and disguises contrary to the usual run of social and economic meanings: a moment which never appears in the London theatre. As Le Roy Ladurie and Natalie Zemon Davis have indicated, such social inversion in early modern Europe unleashed energies which were not only ludic but also violent – and, as *The Rover* suggests, the concerns of carnival in capitalist economy inevitably refer back to the economic and social strictures and hierarchies of the non-carnival, quotidian society.[23]

Carnival offers the three main female characters, Florinda, Valeria, and Hellena, a chance to make their own destiny. Hellena, the youngest, is to go to a nunnery, and Florinda is promised against her will to Don Antonio; but the carnival's disguises and social fluidity allow them to pursue their own sexual (and, in Hellena's case, economic) motives without the controlling presences of their father or brother, Don Pedro. It also permits the exposure of Don Antonio as an unfaithful lover. The cost of their disguises – as gypsies, and in Hellena's case as a page – is that their status as chaste young women of quality is no longer made visible in their dress; and in abandoning the protections of this status, they become, as Ned Blunt puts it of Florinda, 'females' which a man may 'get into his possession' by economic or violent means. The female figures attempt to shape the world of disguised carnival signification in the image of their desires; similarly, they are themselves constituted as signs to be read and misread.

Are they gypsies, prostitutes, or women of quality? Even the audience may sometimes be confused: and this unreadability can be interpreted in two different ways. On the one hand, it might appear that the play proposes an essential chastity or high-value femininity which, although concealed, is nevertheless available to be seen by those who have appropriate social values. On the other hand, the unreadability of women as signs of either prostitution or chastity might be supposed to mean that, whatever their status, they are involved in marketing themselves as sexual commodities, and where then is the much-vaunted difference between the chaste woman and the whore?

This ambivalence of carnival disguise is central to the play. The male figures are to an extent represented as comic or heroic in terms of their ability quickly and accurately to read the signs of a situation even when such signs are concealed; and the audience is also involved in this game because they, too, are posed the problems of recognizing the disguises of figures and understanding their meanings.[24] At the start of the carnival, 'Women drest like Curtezans, with Papers pinn'd to their Breasts, and Baskets of Flowers in their Hands' (Summers. i. I. ii. 18) cross the stage. Blunt, the country nobleman from Essex, and Willmore, who has just disembarked from one of Charles Stuart's ships, wonder about the event:

BLUNT. 'Sheartlikins, what have we here!
FREDERICK. Now the game begins.
WILLMORE. Fine pretty creatures! May a stranger have leave to look and love? What's here – *Roses for every Month*! *(Reads the Paper)*
BLUNT. Roses for every Month! what means that?
BELVILLE. They are, or wou'd have you think they're Curtezans, who here in *Naples* are to be hir'd by the Month.

(Summers, i. I. ii. 19)

Blunt is incomprehending and incurious, interested primarily in the women's bodies; Willmore is willing to go along with the metaphor, reading only the labels (he comments, 'Pray where do these Roses grow? I would fain plant some of 'em in a Bed of mine'). However, Frederick calls attention to the disguise as being part of the game of carnival, and Belville points to the ambiguity of feminine dress, which may disguise 'truth', in the important sense of socio-economic status. With the exception – perhaps – of Willmore's, these reactions prefigure the ability of each of the male characters to use the carnival period productively to gain sexual and financial satisfaction; so that its outcome is tied to their ability to read the ambiguity and instability of carnival signs, and particularly, the signs on women's bodies.

Blunt pursues a 'great lady'; in fact, the prostitute Lucetta, who robs him of everything he has, including his clothes. She has him dropped – presumably through the stage trapdoor – into a sewer in which he wanders almost naked for a long time. Belville, though apparently a good reader of signs, is repeatedly unable to recognize Florinda, who is therefore able to test him and organize a sexual assignation with him in her garden at night.

While Blunt is stripped naked as a sign of his own stupidity, Willmore never participates in carnival disguise. In combination with his name ('will' 'more'), this attribute invites us to read him as a figure of perpetual excess who has simply happened to coincide with a seasonal moment of transformation. He is the romantic lead, and recent productions of the play have taken him very much at his own word when he tells us, 'I'm no tame sigher, but a rampant Lion in the Forest' (Summers, i. I. ii. 19), or, 'I must, like chearful Birds, sing in all Groves, | And Perch on every Bough' (Summers, i. v. i. 86). But it is worth remembering that these associations are his own overstatement. Indeed, it is Willmore who sustains the complications of the plots which keep the lovers apart. He does this not by understanding situations: rather, in pursuit of sex he repeatedly misreads them and makes tactical mistakes. At one point Belville is in disguise as Don Antonio, and Pedro is on the brink of calling a priest to marry him to Florinda at once. Willmore rushes up to Belville and embraces him, causing him to drop his vizard and be revealed to Don Pedro, Florinda's brother – and the plan is ruined.

While Willmore's monomaniac desire to 'score' sexually is used by the plot to frustrate the other lovers' desires, the figure of Angelica illuminates the different ways in which the male figures understand signs. Willmore has been unable to afford the courtesan Angelica Bianca, who charges a thousand crowns for a month of her sexual company (computed on a four-day working week). Don Pedro (Florinda's brother) and Don Antonio (Florinda's lover and intended) both seek to spend their money on her. Blunt initially exclaims against whoring and then asks if she would 'trust' – be willing to take credit.

Angelica Bianca acts initially as a sign of desire. She is

advertised by three pictures, and Willmore makes her acquaintance by attempting to steal one of them, treating the signs as commodities to be gained for himself. Untouched by love, her ability to commodify herself as a desired object answering masculine wishes makes her wealthy. Even more than Sylvia, in Behn's later *Love Letters*, she is a 'fair charmer' who, even more directly than Sylvia or Miranda in *The Fair Jilt* (discussed in Chapter 4), enters the cash economy. As her Brave says, 'This is a Trade, Sir, that cannot thrive by Credit' (Summers, i. II. i. 31); it depends on her physical and psychic ability to turn herself into the answer to all men's desires, and into a sign on which desire can focus, and it is appropriate that, as the ever-receding object of desire, she is represented by multiple images. In watching her, too, the audience was also watching that other commodified object of desire – an actress playing a sexually freighted role. Like an actress, Angelica has reflected back men's desires without desiring herself. The importance of this ability for psychic and economic survival is thrown into relief when she loses it.

Angelica falls for Willmore: 'I never lov'd before, tho' oft a Mistress' (Summers, i. II. ii. 40). At first she realizes he does not believe her: 'I find you cannot credit me' (Summers, i. II. ii. 40) – but she also becomes entirely fixed in a posture of jealous, non-economic desire, and is immediately susceptible to its deceits. Desiring instead of figuring desire, she pursues Willmore, spends money on him, and, like Arnolphe in Molière's *The School for Wives*, is even unlucky enough to tell him the identity of Hellena, his 'Gipsy', a girl of quality and worth 200,000 crowns, unwittingly adding this financial incentive to her rival's youth, wit, and expertise in disguise. As Willmore puts it, 'Ha, my Gipsy worth two hundred thousand crowns! – oh how I long to be with her' (Summers, i. IV. ii. 71). Thus, paradoxically, Hellena is able temporarily to catch Willmore by virtue of shape-shifting and by declaring her nature as the same as his – 'Inconsistent' – while the woman who declares her constancy becomes the economically abused and slighted lover. Hellena's very desirability is figured in her mastery of disguise, her ability not to be herself or remain long in any one identity; she appears to Willmore as gypsy, page, and herself, and her acquisition of the ability to change shape just as Angelica loses it tips the balance fatally against the courtesan-turned-true-lover.

The play ends with the marriage of Hellena, which also allows her – or perhaps Willmore – to claim an inheritance which might otherwise have been kept by her brother. Before this happens, Angelica enters the realms of disguise for one last time, to confront the faithless Willmore. She gains entry to the place where the English are staying, rips off her masquer's costume, and threatens him with a gun, temporarily assuming the role of a masculine outlaw who is beyond the law yet true to vows made. Her violent attempt fails; she is no longer able successfully to assume a disguise. And her disarming follows upon and contrasts with the spectacular and violent implications of disguise offered to us in the previous scene, in which the disguised Florinda therefore comes to the brink of being raped by her brother. Angelica is not hidden; but, because of her status as a courtesan, this renders her as vulnerable as Florinda's carnival disguise makes her.

The scene of Florinda's near-rape, in which the comic complication reaches a climax, paradoxically offers an exciting drama of 'woman-in-peril' while also indicating very clearly the dangerous potential of the carnival disguise. Disguised, Florinda flees from her brother's amorous glances into the house of the English, where she is found by the near-naked Blunt. Still unable to read the signs, he in turn regards her as a gift upon whom as an example he can wreak his righteous revenge on womankind:

> BLUNT. A fine lady-like Whore to cheat me thus without affording me a Kindness for my Money, a Pox light on her, I shall never be reconciled to the Sex more, she has made me as faithless as a Physician, as uncharitable as a Church-man, and as ill-natured as a Poet, O how I'll use all Womenkind hereafter! What wou'd I give to have one of 'em within my reach now! Any Mortal thing in Petticoats, kind Fortune, send me.
>
> (Summers, i. IV. iii. 81)

And at this point Florinda appears. Soon all the English and Don Pedro are disputing who shall rape her first. They draw swords to decide, and Don Pedro's long 'Toledo' blade entitles him to first place. Thus, if we 'freeze' the action at this comic climax, a very few minutes before the final resolution of the comedy in the marriages of the three pairs of lovers, what we find is still a rich seam of potential violence and anguish.

Blunt (baptized by sewage) and Angelica (tortured by her loving fixity) are in search of violent revenge. In Blunt's case the motive is an injury made possible by a misreading of disguise; in Angelica's, her change from desired object to desiring subject has left her fixed in love. She is able to read the signs of Willmore's unfaithfulness, but is unable to change her own desires. Florinda, disguised and therefore of no recognizable social status, is about to be gang-raped, with her brother to violate her first. In seeking to enjoy and benefit from the carnival, the women so far have succeeded only in testing Belville's fidelity; and Don Antonio, through his attempt to purchase the now obsessed Angelica, has exposed himself to Don Pedro and to Belville as an unfaithful lover to Florinda. Interesting Willmore in a sexual encounter can hardly count as a triumph on the women's side.

We might ask, as we did of the beating of Sensure in *The City Heiress*, is this comedy? If it is, we must once more acknowledge that comedy licenses an audience to laugh at physical violence. If this is the case, we may ask precisely what social and cultural work comedy is doing in representing such moments as funny – sometimes side-splittingly funny – when in another genre we would find them violent and dangerous (as in the attempted rape of Belvidera in Thomas Otway's near-contemporary tragedy, *Venice Preserv'd*). Such ambiguity is open to resolution, of course, in its acting-out either as a climax of laughter or as dangerous and confusing.

In judging how far the play questions the possibility of stable and disinterested relations between the sexes, much depends on how much weight we place on the closure in marriage present in the subsequent scenes, and how we choose to interpret the situation of Angelica. Is the critic Mary Ann O'Donnell correct in suggesting that the final moments of the play produce classic comic closure, tying up all the loose ends, and endorsing the heterosexual pairing of marriage, at least when it is freely chosen?[25] Angelica departs thwarted, transformed from an object of desire into a desiring and fixed subject. Don Pedro realizes that he was about to rape his sister. Carnival, by loosening the social fixity of the virgins, enables them to use disguise and desire to their own ends – but only at the potential cost of suffering economic dangers, and a physical and sexual violence which almost culminates in brother–sister rape. If the play is ambivalent about the power of law, as in marriage, to fix desire, the end of the comedy undermines any such closure or sense that everything is tidied up. This unease is reinforced, I would suggest, by the scene of Hellena's marriage vows, during which we might remember Willmore's speech, even at gunpoint, about his inability to be faithful. Hellena, still a witty inconstant, nevertheless demands marriage to obtain her dowry. Their courtship dialogue goes as follows:

> WILLMORE. Hold, hold, no Bugg Words, Child, Priest and Hymen...Marriage is...[a] certain Bane to Love...I could be content to turn Gipsy...to have the Pleasure to working that great Miracle of making a Maid a Mother... and if I miss, I'll lose my Labour.
> HELLENA. And if you do not lose what shall I get? A Cradle full of Noise and Mischief, with a pack of Repentance at my Back...
> WILLMORE. I can teach thee to weave a true Love's Knot better.
> HELLENA. So can my Dog.
>
> (Summers, i. v. i. 100–1)

Thus the alternatives to marriage for a woman are very fully delineated before the contract. What remains in question is how, exactly, Hellena's lot with Willmore could be altered by giving him her fortune which would otherwise have either followed her to a nunnery or have been kept by her brother. In *The Rover*, a number of loose ends complicate the extent to which marriage can be seen as a 'happy' or permanent ending. And when the popularity of this play provoked Behn to write *The Rover II*, it is notable that Willmore remains fancy-free – we are told that Hellena died at sea after a mere month of marriage.

The audience, then, are not given enough information to come to a certain decision about the desirability of the union of the 'Rover' and Hellena. Indeed, it would be misleading to consider the questions raised by this marriage solely within the terms of tying up the plot without taking into account the significance of disguise, and the need to read signs throughout the play. How are we to understand disguised and undisguised figures? The metadramatic aspect of the play, too – including the use of asides and occasions when the audience knows more than the actors – requires us to attend to the audience's own interpretation of the play. The actresses' bodies – being simultaneously revealed and ambiguous, in a plot during which one actress might play a courtesan turned true lover, while another plays a virgin disguised as a prostitute – come to signify both the pleasures of desire and transformation and the need, both economic and social, to distinguish and interpret, if that desire is to be made economically productive. So at the end of the play, though the characters might be undisguised to each other, the audience is still uncertain about the meaning of the marriage between Hellena and Willmore. And, as Willmore suggests, marriage is the end of carnival.

BEHN'S DRAMA: SOME CONCLUSIONS

Behn's comedies of the late 1670s to late 1680s put before their audiences the political, sexual, and economic issues of the period. As suggested in the Introduction, the plays both articulate and comment upon contemporary polemical positions including Behn's own Tory line. It would be possible to argue that while they express the Tory ideology of the period they comment critically on Behn's own social and sexual ideologies: one might point to the punishment of the nasty old men as political satire, and the way in which her plays are repeatedly equivocal about the benefits for women of marriage which often ends not in the formation of happy couples, but in the re-formation of happy unmarried couples – couples emerge from the dissolution of unhappy partnerships.

It is certainly clear that Behn's plays intervene in both these areas. But in offering a historicized reading of Behn's plays this chapter has suggested that, as so often in Behn's writing, the situation is more complicated, more contradictory, than this. Yes, her plays do articulate support for Charles II and James II. Yes, they do suggest that women's sexual freedom is desirable. But they also focus our attention on the old Commonwealthsmen as a kind of fascinating enemy. And both Wilding's syphilitic libertinism and the violent beating of the puritan Sensure in *The City Heiress* suggest that the political and the sexual are bound up together for Behn, and that sexual freedom is only to be claimed by and for certain women – women who, like Lady Fancy, Lady Julia Fulbank, and others, take up pro-Tory positions.

In Behn's writing we are never far from contradictory impulses and potentials. Critics have tried to make coherent sense out of her plays by having recourse to two things: her gender, and her prefatory material – the prologues, prefaces, and dedications. We might remember that Behn's contemporaries attempted to explain her plays by calling her a whore. Contemporary critics, like Langdell, look instead for reified images of 'Behn the woman' in the plays; other critics attempt to trace the 'true' Behn in the prefaces. Critics have seen both as lying safely outside the text and therefore offering reliable and non-contradictory evidence. However, of course, Behn's gender was textualized, not only by critics but repeatedly by Behn herself. The image of a woman dramatist is positively fetishized in her repeated references to it; her sex is constantly referred to as part of a sales pitch in prologues, epilogues, and prefaces, offering the reader the frisson of an almost-forbidden commodity – a sexual–political comedy, by a woman. And the prefaces, too, although they do offer some explicit comments on the gender of the writer, also need to be seen in relation to the debates of the moment. Far from being – at last – simple statements of what Behn *really* thought, we might understand the prefaces as addressing the material and ideological circumstances which produced plays (and prefaces), first on stage and then as printed texts.

A case in point is Behn's preface to *The Lucky Chance*. Even this text was produced at a particular moment when the debates on female authorship and on female spectatorship coincided, and in itself it is far from unambiguous about the reputation of the woman dramatist. As we have seen, the female authorship of these plays was controversial: a twin critical obsession emerged with women as writers and women as spectators. Defences of the representation of sexuality and what we might think of as sexually explicit scenes in comedy were carried by Sir Charles Sedley's *Bellamira* (1687) and Behn's *The Lucky Chance* (1686). In response to strictures on female spectatorship and authorship, Behn noted that it was not 'as if ... the Ladys were oblig'd to hear Indecencys only from their Pens and Plays'. Moreover, she ties female spectatorship and authorship together, noting that such scenes 'are never taken Notice of' if 'a Man writ them'.

It was in the context of this debate that the preface to *The Lucky Chance* delivered Behn's longest piece of writing on women's authorship:

> If I must not, because of my Sex, have this Freedom [to write], but that you will usurp all to your selves; I lay down my Quill, and you shall hear no more of me, no, not so much as to make Comparison, because I will be kinder to my Brothers of the Pen, than they have been to a defenceless Woman; for I am not content to write for a Third day only. I value fame as much as if I had been born a *Hero*; and if you rob me of that, I can retire from the ungrateful World, and scorn its fickle favours.

At first reading this seems like a straightforward defence of women's writing; and this is how it is often read by critics. However, a second glance throws up some contradictions. Is the pose that of a shrinking violet or a woman claiming equality with men? Does the text claim innocence or superiority? The prose oscillates between vulnerability and power. Indeed, 'fame' can suggest both the posterity of success as a writer, and that of a woman's high reputation for charity and chastity.

So even this apparently straightforward defence of writing both seeks and eschews masculine approval, claiming and disclaiming virtue in the ambiguous use of 'fame'. If the plays, as I have argued, are marked by positions which are in part undermined by the way they focus our attention, or offer for our pleasure, very complicated workings-out of the relationship between politics and sexuality, then the prefaces, prologues, epilogues, and biographical anecdotes surrounding Behn are also complex structures of meaning.

However, this is not a reason to discard them, any more than it is a reason to close down the contradictions on an imagined fixed point called 'Aphra' or 'woman'. In my readings of her plays I have tried to offer a turning-away from biographical analysis towards a reading which recognizes that the ideologies of the society Behn lived and worked in were themselves highly contradictory. For example, women were not supposed to publish or write professionally, yet the fact that a text was written by a woman was, clearly, a marketing pull. Such texts do not simply give back to their society meanings and stereotypes as they found them but, again also in a contradictory way, offer a particular perspective on or critique of those meanings as they circulate.

And this rich field of contradictory impulses is particularly marked in Behn's political and other comedies. In the prose fiction, to which the last third of this book is devoted, contradictions operate in a very different way. As I shall suggest, in the short fiction the activity of the reader is often the place where contradictions begin to work themselves out and, just as audiences for the plays needed to be alert to the multiple connections between sexuality, finance, and politics, readers of the fiction need to listen for whether or not we are being told the truth. Or whether the narrator is up to something altogether more manipulative.

4

Fiction

SHORTER FICTION

'No more Truth than a Narrative' says a character in *Sir Timothy Treat-All* in 1682 (Summers, ii. II. i. 245). This was the year in which the King's and Duke's theatres amalgamated, reducing opportunities for staging plays. The situation seems to have prompted Behn to turn her attention to print. At first she published poetry, turning to prose narrative towards the end of the 1680s. She published both very long texts, like the multi-volume *Love Letters between a Nobleman and his Sister*, and fictions of about the length of a twentieth-century short story, which appeared in collections. That such stories were popular is suggested by their sheer quantity, though here there is space to discuss only four.

In the second half of the seventeenth century a market for prose developed which was in many ways an extension of elements of bookselling already present. This market is often characterized by twentieth-century critics as signalling the beginning of the novel – the dominant genre in the eighteenth century. Certainly during the 1680s prose narrative was both saleable and suspect because of its ability simultaneously to mimic truth (a novelistic quality) and to offer romance plotting. The romance has a long history, but had most recently been used as a commentary of courts and politics which also offered layered stories of shepherds, disguise, kings, and princes, as in Lady Mary Wroth's *Urania*. Behn's shorter fiction, just like her very long *Love Letters* and the novella-length *Oroonoko*, appeared at this transitional moment when 'truth' or 'history' and 'invention' or 'romance' existed together in fictions. It would, therefore, be misleading to approach her stories as we do twentieth-century short stories; bearing the legacy of romance, they work with the powerful popularity of scandal and travel narrative, and with an early modern sense of the possibilities open to the heroine.

In such fictions it is impossible to make a clear, formal demarcation between strategies typical of the long multi-layered stories known as romances or of novels. For example, Behn's stories 'The Unfortunate Happy Lady' and *The Fair Jilt* combine techniques characteristic of both romance and novel – they take romance plots, shorten them, and situate them in an economically and morally indeterminate novelistic world of materiality, exigency, and caprice. The stories abound in accidents and coincidences and repeatedly focus on sequestered women, whether in convents or in their father's houses; but they also focus on urban settings, money, and, sometimes, politics.[1] Short fictions at this period are marked by political concerns, and include allusions to such matters as the Exclusion crisis, the question of vows, and the status of Venice as a republic. Unlike the eighteenth-century domestic fiction which was to follow, Behn's fiction often encodes an implicit or explicit political dimension.

An important element taken up in Behn's stories from romance is femino-centric narrative – that is, narrative which focuses on the experiences of a female protagonist. This section examines two different treatments of women, and women's desires, in Behn's stories, and discusses the question and positioning of desire in relation both to the reader and to the female protagonist.

In contrast to the female protagonists of late-eighteenth-century novels such as Fanny Burney's *Evelina*, many of Behn's figures are overtly and actively involved in the world. They want things. And, as Peter Brooks has convincingly argued, the desire of a protagonist for fame, fortune, and recognition is a crucial force in making a story. It acts like an engine, producing narrative from the 'wanting' of the central figure.[2] However, in concentrating on the male protagonists of the nineteenth-century novel, Brooks and other critics tend to ignore precisely the problem which Behn's stories investigate – how can a story be told in which a female protagonist is positioned in relation to such desires for fortune and material possessions?

One way is to characterize a female protagonist as innocent of all desire, and to encourage the reader, through the events in the narrative, to want everything to 'work out alright'. In such stories the heroines are rewarded. For example, the narrator of the enigmatic story 'The Black Lady' describes the central figure, Bellamora, as the 'Innocent (I must not say foolish) one' (Todd, iii. 316), who is thereby distanced from the implicitly wise reader. The 'innocent' (though pregnant and unmarried) protagonist comes to London in search of a place to have her baby. By good fortune, the trunk she mislays is returned and she goes to lodge at the house where the sister of her child's father is staying. Fondlove, the father, is brought to town, but the landlady and his sister keep him from the 'lady'. The reader knows all of this; the protagonist knows none of it. Instead:

> She [the landlady] told her that things were miscarried, and she fear'd, lost; that she had but little Money herself, and if the Overseers of the Poor (justly so call'd from their over-looking 'em) should have the least Suspicion of a strange and unmarried Person, who was entertain'd in her House big with Child, and so neare her time as Bellamora was, she should be troubled, if they could not give Security to the Parish of twenty or thirty Pounds, that they should not suffer by her, which she cou'd not; or otherwise she must be sent to the House of Correction, and her Child to a Parish-Nurse. This Discourse, one may imagine, was very dreadful to someone of her Youth, Beauty, Education, Family and Estate.

> (Todd, iii. 319)

Bellamora thus hears the likely negative outcome of her various imprudent actions. The text also calls attention to the contrasting likely fate of Bellamora and the other 'black lady' of the narrative, a cat. The cat, like Bellamora, is searching for a safe place to give birth. But she, unlike Bellamora, is untroubled by the law. The big city and the law give shelter to the cat because they have no interest in exploiting or policing feline sexuality; but the young woman is saved only by great good fortune.

The narration, keeping up a distance between what the reader knows and what the protagonist understands to be the case, emphasizes the good fortune of the circumstances which saves her from the all-too-likely disaster. The comparisons between the fate of the woman and the cat, and of the outcome in the story as opposed to the likely outcome in life, are left implicit. As readers, our desire for the protagonist to achieve material security is mediated and manipulated by a narrator who negotiates between the version heard by the innocent (or foolish) Bellamora and what we know to be the case. The reader is given the pleasure of knowing that our protagonist will, in fact, get what we want for her. Thus, in this story of Behn's, unlike some others, the desire in the text is the reader's, not Bellamora's own.

The emphasis on the reader's role in wanting things to happen to a passive female figure recurs in the story 'The Unfortunate Happy Lady: A True History' in which, once again, a likely disaster is redeemed. It is 'an account of the uncommon Villany of a Gentleman...practis'd upon his Sister' (Todd, iii. 365) On the death of their father the brother and heir runs wild: 'in less than a Twelve-Month, he was forc'd to return to his seat in the Country, to Mortgage a part of his estate of a Thousand Pounds a year' (Todd, iii. 365) in order to begin to repay huge debts. Rather than pay her portion, her brother dumps our heroine at a brothel where, he tells her, she is to be educated by a wise older woman.

However, in rewriting this potentially quasi-pornographic narrative of how a woman becomes a whore, a story of the sort both found in earlier romances and to be utilized by Defoe and Cleland, Philadelphia is rescued by the man who has paid to have her maidenhead, one Gracelove. Having pursued her into a bedroom ('the proper Field for our Dispute'), he becomes convinced at the last minute of her innocence. He informs her, 'You are in a naughty House, and that old Beldam is a rank Procuress, to whom I am to give Two hundred Guineas for your Maidenhead', and delivers her 'out of the Jaws of Perdition' into the care of one Fairlaw.

From this point, without any intervention of her own desire beyond compliance, fortune and judicious marriage elevate her to a position where she has more than enough control over her circumstances. First, Gracelove proposes. She refuses, saying 'she could not consent to marry him, who had so plentiful a Fortune, and she had nothing but her innocence' (Todd, iii. 378). The reader, of course, desires this marriage, but, just as it is about to take place, Gracelove is whisked away on a voyage and soon presumed dead. The next to propose is old Fairlaw, 'not forgetting...to let her know that his Widow...would be worth above thirty thousand Pounds in ready money'. Needless to say, our heroine marries him for his good qualities – it is the reader, rather than the grieving heroine, who is delighted to find her a young, immensely wealthy widow after a mere four months of marriage. The heroine's purity is maintained by her lack of interest in lucre.

From here it is but a short step to the return of Gracelove and the rescue of her brother. She finds her old lover destitute and is able to give him a horse (a gift which suggests a symbolic return to his manhood). She even takes him to her house and proposes marriage to him as she dismisses three other lovers. The brother has been suitably punished; he has 'learnt the art of Peg-making' in debtor's prison, where Philadelphia's charitable agent discovers him. She rescues him from prison and marries him to her first husband's daughter. And so she wins all, together with the moral high ground.

Obviously, such a story gains some of its fascination from the very way in which the female protagonist achieves success. Moreover, no desire or grossly materialistic impulse is attributed to her; the mediation of the narrator ensures that it is the reader who wants the rewards of wealth and status to be conferred on her. If the story is one of wish-fulfilment, then the wishes are again firmly situated in the reader rather than the heroine, whose only desire is a chaste, marital one for Gracelove. The story licenses this desire and organizes its fulfilment as coinciding with worldly success for the heroine. Nevertheless, even in this fiction the reader can recall the transgressive circumstances of their first meeting in the whorehouse and marvel at the working-out of his wild desire into economically productive wedlock.

As a glance at the protagonists in Behn's fictions makes clear, the number of things a late-seventeenth-century female prose protagonist might legitimately desire was severely restricted. Many desires were, in themselves, almost automatically considered transgressive when ascribed to a woman. For example, a female figure may want to marry (as does Hellena in *The Rover*), but social or economic ambitions beyond this are problematic or blameworthy in women. So, where Peter Brooks sees ambition as the metaphor for desire and the engine of narrative incident in the nineteenth-century novel, and writes of the typical male protagonist as 'a bundle of desires', Behn's seventeenth-century female protagonists tend to be positioned differently, and in 'The Black Lady' and 'The Unfortunate Happy Lady' the drive for the acquisition of money and power are located outside the central figure.

Meanwhile, we, the readers, are organized as bourgeois good-housekeepers whose desire for economic security is coded into the heroine's success, while the protagonist is kept hygienically separate from base longings and social ambitions.

But some of the protagonists of Behn's feminocentric narratives do have desires, and this brings with it rather different narrative organization. All the things such a central figure might wish for – money, fame, sexual experience, autonomy, power – develop negative moral connotations in female subjects. Yet, as Behn's narrator in *The History of the Nun* suggests, women do have such desires, albeit concealed by modesty: 'women are taught, by the Lives of Men, to live up to all their Vices, and are become almost as inconstant; and 'tis but Modesty that makes the difference' (Todd, iii. 212). The desiring female protagonists, like Miranda in *The Fair Jilt*, approximate more closely to Brooks's sense of the desiring male protagonist whose ambitions motivate the text; but they are posed as problematic figures, and the stories offer the reader a shifting and complicated position.

Desire, in the sense of sexual desire rather than desire for security, is encoded by these stories as rendering women vulnerable to social and economic disaster. In the politically loaded 'The Dumb Virgin' a romance instigated by two sisters under disguise at a masquerade causes not only an illicit sexual relationship, but accidental incest. We see that, while sexual desire is dangerous to the female lover, economic and social desires tend to transform them, as in the cases of *The Fair Jilt* and *The History of the Nun*, into agents, storytellers, manipulators – and criminals. Behn's texts deal with the relationship between the reader and such 'criminals' in complex ways.

The power to use words persuasively and to tell a story which is believed and manipulates the hearer's desire is an attribute of the more desiring, active, and calculating of the central figures in Behn's short fiction. Unlike the central figure of 'The Black Lady', rendered happy by coincidental plot details, or that of the 'Unfortunate Happy Lady' who achieves control without effort, Miranda, in *The Fair Jilt*, is capable of manipulating language. Interestingly, her story claims that 'every Circumstance, to a Tittle, is truth' (indeed, the failed execution of Prince Tarquino was recorded in the *London Gazette* of 28–31 May 1666, when Behn was in Antwerp). This claim to veracity is combined with a duplicitous complexity of narration.

As the story opens a young girl, Miranda, lives semi-sequestered in a kind of temporary orders 'taken up by the best Persons in the Town'. The story charts her moral, sexual, and material progress from apparently innocent girl to plotter who deceives her husband and attacks her sister. Miranda falls in love with a young monk, whose own story, present in an embedded narrative, is one of failed communication, intercepted letters, and frustration. She approaches him in the confessional: 'Behold her now deny'd, refus'd and defeated, with all her pleading Youth, Beauty, Tears and Knees, imploring, as she lay, holding fast to his *Scapular*, and embracing his feet' (Todd, iii. 28). But what seems a partly comic attempt at seduction is soon transformed when Miranda realizes that his refusal is absolute:

> throwing her self...into the Confessing-Chair, and violently pulling the young Friar into her lap, she elevated her Voice to such a Degree, in crying out *Help, Help! A Rape! Help, Help!* that she was heard all over the Church.
>
> (Todd, iii. 24)

Unable to seduce him in the confessional, Miranda cries out that he has assaulted her; her agency enables her to re-establish control over circumstances, and her account of the struggle in the confessional, itself a symbolic location of truth and knowledge, is at first accepted. In the believability of her version of events, in the way it finds currency, Behn's story points towards the way control of the narration of events confers on the teller an ability to control their meaning, a point already discussed in Chapter 2. So Behn's desiring protagonists become makers and controllers of meaning, even if in order to keep those desires hidden.

In 'The Unfortunate Happy Lady' the reader desired the happy outcome; but those of Behn's stories with an active central female figure provide a more complex set of choices and ambivalences. On the one hand, the heroine is the focus of all our interest, but, on the other hand, she is criminal. *The Fair Jilt* foregrounds the problematic nature of the reader's relationship to Miranda. Having married, attempted to murder her sister, caused the death of a page, and likely to cause the death of her husband, Miranda breaks her silence and 'confesses'. At this point the reader discovers that she or he is in a limited position because Miranda confesses to a number of entirely new crimes. She:

Confess'd all her Life, all the Lewdness of her Practices with several Princes and great Men, besides her Lusts with people that served her and others in mean Capacity: And lastly, the whole Truth of the young Friar; and how she had drawn her Page, and the Prince her husband, to this design'd Murder of her Sister.

(Todd, iii. 42)

This surprises the reader by making it clear that the story we are reading of Miranda is only one of several possible stories of her sexual and financial agency, in all of which she seems to have played the role of desiring subject. The narrator has chosen not to disclose all these possible plot-lines to us, bringing forward concealed narrative material to confirm the power of telling the story. Confession is used within the narrative as an apparent signal of repentance and change but, simultaneously, it alerts the reader to the power of narration to produce meaning both by ordering and by withholding information.

While the confessional document brings about Francisco's release, it does not cause Miranda's downfall, but foregrounds her control over her circumstances and successful concealment of facts. Moreover, rather than administering any 'punishment', the narrative allows her to repeat this 'trick' when she lives out the remainder of her days under the protection of the prince's father, who looks upon her as his son's financial benefactress. (We might compare the sanctioned separations at the end of Behn's comedies.)

Of course, in Peter Brooks's terms, Miranda is a protagonist who can indeed be described as a 'bundle of desires'. Miranda is endowed with 'ungoverned' sexual, social, and financial passions – she seeks the prizes which the 'Unfortunate Happy Lady' is awarded by the narrative without attempting to gain them. As the narrator tells us:

I'll prove to you the strong Effects of Love in some unguarded and ungovern'd Hearts; where it rages beyond Inspirations of a *God all soft and gentle*, and reigns more like *a Fury from hell*.

(Todd, iii. 9)

Part of the pleasure of reading about Miranda is that she is this transgressive subject, with 'wild Desires'. The narrator tells us that she is not virtuous at the opening of the narrative – she merely has 'the Reputation of being retir'd from the world' (Todd, iii. 75). But it is not until she becomes an active and criminal agent in her own destiny that we see her as both wicked and powerful.

Yet she remains the focus of the reader's interest and narrative desire, and the reader's enjoyment of her exploits is not wholly undermined by the close of the story. Notably, Miranda is not punished at the end of the narrative by deprivation, only by retirement: a sharp contrast with many later eighteenth- or particularly nineteenth-century femino-centric fictions, whose ambitious female protagonists are punished for their desires, and are often literally turned inside out to expose the lurking evil under their powerful beauty and rhetoric. An obvious example is the smallpox which scars Madame de Merteuil in Laclos's *Les Liaisons dangereuses*, reinforcing her status as an outcast from society at the end of the novel, even though it is her scheming and ambition which have provided the reader with virtually all the narrative pleasure of that text.

Thus, within a femino-centric narrative, the active pursuit by female protagonists of social, sexual, and economic improvement is both problematic and fascinating. Behn's stories negotiate this problem through the shifting sympathies and knowledge of the protagonist, reader, and narrator. In one set of stories the protagonist is entirely innocent, but in others, as she becomes a desiring subject, she is 'found out' as a criminal. The movement from economic, social, and sexual passivity into agency, the moment at which such agency is uncovered or exposed, is one to which these short fictions return.

The Fair Jilt offers us a central figure who is a knowing sexual and financial agent; but another story, *The History of the Nun; or, the Fair Vow-Breaker*, narrates the 'finding-out' of such agency. This woman is in part already compromised by her choice of love over a convent and having made her second marriage for 'means' (in order to survive). When Isabella's first husband, reported dead in battle, unexpectedly reappears while her second husband is away hunting, Isabella is revealed for the first time – to herself and to the audience – as an economic and socially ambitious subject, and as a criminal:

> In one moment she ran over a thousand Thoughts. She finds, by his Return, she is not only expos'd to all the Shame imaginable; to all the Upbraiding, on his part, when he shall know she is marry'd to another; but all the Fury and Rage of *Villenoys*, and the scorn of the Town, who will look on her as an Adulteress: She sees *Henault* poor,

and knew, she must fall from all the Glory and Tranquility she had for
five Happy Years Triumph'd in: in which Time, she had known no
sorrow or Care, tho' she had endur'd a thousand with *Henault*.

(Todd, iii. 249)

From this recognition of desire for economic safety and social
security – a recognition forced by the threat of their removal after
they have been achieved, apparently with minimal effort – it is but a
short step to full agency and dual murder: she kills both husbands.
Once desire and economic gain are exposed as driving forces in
Isabella, she becomes an agent in her destiny. Once discovered as
agents, these protagonists also become planners, staging their own
stories and manipulating language to suit their purposes.

The complex relationships set up amongst narrator, protagonist,
and reader render Behn's stories enigmatic. At times they are like
riddles, or dilemmas that resist moral (rather than narrative)
solutions. As a reader we want to know what happens. We might
be in suspense (what will happen between X and Y?) or curious
(is the first husband really dead, or will he return to disturb the
second marriage?).[3] But the desire to know, to read on, can also be
seen in terms of shifting patterns of relationship between reader,
narrator, and protagonist. Importantly, each of Behn's many
stories employs a narrator who is able to intervene and organize
the reader's desire in particular ways. Such narrative desire, basic
to the reading process, can be analysed in terms of what the main
figure wants, what we want for them, and what the genre leads us
to expect will happen. For example, the reader may well wish that
the character whose desires are being exposed to us will get what
she wants, not only in terms of acquiring a thing or person she
desires but also in terms of reaching an overall goal. Thus, the role
of the narrator structures the reader's own desire and pleasure: as
Ross Chambers notes, 'stories are not separable from their *telling*'.
And in some of the texts the 'telling' makes us, the readers, the
engines of desire for the protagonist; in others, as suggested
above, the protagonists are found out as themselves desiring
subjects.

What the stories do not provide is neat generic moralizations.
They do not necessarily end with punishment; and in this they sit
at ideological and generic borderlines, ideologically and generically indeterminate – they are neither romances nor, exactly, short

stories. Like romance, they do not insist on compensatory punishment, but neither do they offer its long interwoven stories. Nor do they conform to our twentieth-century expectations of the novel. Rather, prose narrative of this period, is able to move between truth claims and to mimic prose genres from fact to romance.

Thus, Behn's fiction, appearing late in her career, forms part of a moment when romance and novelistic techniques combine. The fluidity of codes and kinds of narration offer readers complex and different way of engaging with the desires of female protagonists. At this point the female protagonist may only be coded as innocent or desiring; but prose narrative allows a multiplicity of different endings. What is repeated from story to story is the complexity of the relationship between the reader, the narrator, and the protagonist. As her stories suggest, in the late seventeenth century – at a moment before the dominance of the novel as a form of prose fiction – prose narrative was sophisticated and very flexible, able to manipulate the feelings of the reader and refuse pat moralizations. This complexity recurs in Behn's longer fictions, in both *Oroonoko, or the Royal Slave* and in the next text to be discussed, *Love Letters between a Nobleman and his Sister*.

LOVE LETTERS BETWEEN A NOBLEMAN AND HIS SISTER

As the title suggests, *Love Letters between a Nobleman and his Sister* is the story of a scandalous affair between a nobleman and his wife's sister ('sister' covered both sister and sister-in-law in seventeenth-century terminology), told in the letters between the couple. The 'Argument' tells us more:

> *Philander* cast his eyes upon a young maid, sister to *Mertilla* [his wife], a Beauty, whose early bloom promises wonders when come to perfection...He Loved and languished long...While the young lovely *Silvia* (so we shall call the noble Maid) sight out her hours in the same pain and languishment for *Philander*...After [their] flight these letters were found in their Cabinets...and they are as exactly as possible plac'd in the order they were sent.[5]
>
> (Todd, iv. 10)

But this is only one aspect of the story. In fact, the three-volume fiction is partly epistolary and partly told by a narrator outside the exchange of letters. And the couple involved, Philander and Silvia, are based on contemporary people and events. Indeed, the significance of the transgressive love between brother- and sister-in-law is political as well as marital; the families of the real-life lovers were in opposed political camps. This would have been at least part of the reason that the first audience bought the book, and it is part of what is interesting for a modern reader. But one of the most striking things about the text is the way it explores deceitful eloquence, desire, and shape-changing in sexual and political contexts.

As a very long, partly epistolary fiction interweaving politics and sexual politics, *Love Letters* poses problems for the reader which are not present, or are not so important, in Behn's shorter fiction. Here we may examine the ways in which the text uses the epistolary style to invite the reader to question the power and sincerity of the lovers' persuasive language, and analyse how the adulterous central figures – so evidently anti-heroic, but so intriguing – are made the focus of our sympathetic interest.

For the first readers, as it was published in parts from 1684 to 1687, the interest of the text would have been the connection between the transgressive love and the explosive contemporary political situation. As discussed in the Introduction, Monmouth rebelled against the Roman Catholic James II soon after he took the throne; he was subsequently put to death, and his supporters were punished. This event marked, temporarily, the end of opposition to Stuart rule; after he had defeated Monmouth, James II remained king until he was deposed in 1688. *Love Letters* follows the national political narrative leading up to the rebellion, and deals with events of national significance by approaching them through the scandalous lives of players in the contemporary political field.

The real-life story which the text reworks is the elopement of Lady Henrietta Berkeley with her brother-in-law, Lord Grey of Werke. Werke was a supporter of James, Duke of Monmouth; Lady Henriette Berkeley was an heiress of Tory parentage. Their elopement was therefore a double scandal, both sexual and political. Lady Berkeley was tracked down by her family after her father placed an advertisement in the *London Gazette* offering £200 for her return, but by then she was married to one of Werke's aides and permanently beyond the reach of father and family. In real life, too, Lord Grey of Werke took an increasingly active part in politics and in plotting against the succession of James, Duke of York. He was pardoned by James II after he took part in Monmouth's rebellion, and it is this incident which Behn uses to close her last volume, opening a door on to real life at the moment the text ends with the indication that the situation continues as Philander 'was at last pardoned, kissed the King's hand, and came to Court, in as much splendour as ever, being very well understood by all good men'.

However, the use of real-life events and material does not mean that the text is not a highly wrought and carefully constructed fiction. Rather, it gives the reader at least two ways to read the text – both by following the narrative thread and its twists and turns around the protagonists Silvia and Philander, and at the same time by catching the references to actual political events and seeing how the prism of the fiction refracts their meanings.

The letters and narrative tell an amorous and political story, shaped in part as a romance. The heiress, Silvia, elopes with her sister's husband, Philander. The two families are already on opposing sides of the political divide between supporters of the succession of the king and Cesario, the fictionalized Duke of Monmouth. But, although fiction follows and transforms historical events, we are not simply offered a chronicle of daily life; the text is not news, but a fiction. The whole scene is transposed to France 'in the time of the rebellion of the true Protestant *Huguenot* in Paris'; and many things happen to the lovers in the three volumes which have nothing at all to do with the lives of Berkeley and Werke. In order to move from fiction to fact we need to compare events, a process which operates as a key to lead us, as readers, back into our own real world – outside the fiction, though related to it.

The first readers, particularly, would have enjoyed decoding the secrets of the texts and unlocking the doors between the fictional and real world. Such cross-party, cross-class sexual scandal would obviously have a wide appeal. And the story of a woman's sexual misdemeanour offers potential for manipulation of the reader's empathy and identification as well as occasion for sexual and political satire, a potential which the text astutely exploits, turning the scandal into both moving romance and political satire. Philander is both the 'charming, lovely youth' and politically and sexually 'the most perfidious of his sex'. Thus the fascinating details of the real case can be unlocked, or decoded, in Behn's narrative; but what we read is not so much real-life drama as a narrative shaped by the codes and conventions of romance, scandal, pastoral, and other forms of fiction. Indeed, the very potential of the story to be unlocked, and for readers to have the thrill of making the connections, is a function of its encoding as romance.

However, *Love Letters* is not only of interest because of its treatment of a contemporary scandal, and because it pleased several following generations of readers. The fact that relatively little critical attention has been paid to the text in the twentieth century seems not to be a consequence of its topical significance, but rather an effect of its liminal, or threshold, status as neither exactly epistolary nor narrated, neither romance nor novel, neither news nor history. Like Behn's shorter fiction, it belongs to a cultural moment when the codes of history and romance were being interwoven. Twentieth-century criticism of the novel has tended to see it as evolving towards realism – what Ian Watt called 'the defining characteristic which differentiates the work of the early eighteenth-century novelists from previous fiction', and critics of the eighteenth-century novel have, until recently, tended to marginalize texts which, like *Love Letters*, offer evidence which contradicts that argument. More recently critics such as Michael McKeon have argued that it is unproductive to see the novel as emerging from a gradual suppression of romance elements in favour of verisimilitude and *histoire*. Rather, it is necessary to understand texts from the 1680s as drawing on elements of a range of prose modes and competing ways of writing. At the time, readers and writers were disputing and attempting to define the characteristics which might distinguish novel, news, *histoire*, history, and romance, but, as this very debate suggests, while wishing to discover separable prose genres, they found it hard, even impossible, to distinguish clearly even between fact and fiction. An acknowledgment of this generic complexity in the 1680s enables us to appreciate the discursive complexity of texts like *Love Letters*.[6]

In the 1680s such dual and, to us, contradictory effects were frequently used, and were later developed in the sentimental novel. In *Love Letters* they are created by an overlayering of pastoral and political discourses. As we shall see with *Oroonoko*, claims to veracity and verisimilitude associated with *histoire*, or history, could coexist with elements of romance, such as quest narratives. Ros Ballaster notes, indeed, that *Love Letters* 'doubly articulates the political and the sexual, eroticizing the former while it politicizes the latter'.[7] For the reader, part of the pleasure in this rich mixture was the way these different modes of writing encoded and overlayered each other, moving between 'the arts and politics of love' and 'arms and power'. Thus, the story of the lovers in *Love Letters* is interwoven with political controversy which gradually gains prominence in the narrative: the 'claim to the crown' is set against the 'natural charms' of transgressive love.

The blockbuster qualities of *Love Letters* contrast sharply with Behn's shorter fiction, perhaps the main difference being the use of a topical political story to make a *roman à clef*. But one of the ways this text uses its size, generic instability, and relationship to real life is to offer the reader a prolonged exploration of seductive eloquence, and the power of language and disguise, to ensnare the sexually and politically innocent. In *Love Letters*, as we saw in Chapter 2, there is no 'natural charm' which links eloquence to truth, and we remember the words of Behn's nymph who believed her lover: 'I took in, believ'd, and was undone' (see page 18).

Eloquence and changeability, transformation, can charm and seduce both politically and sexually; but, as the last sentence of *Love Letters* reminds us, there is no guarantee that deceitful eloquence will be 'very well understood by all good men'. How can the reader of a letter accurately estimate its sincerity? How can a reader – either the addressee of the letter or the reader – estimate the relationship between the power of eloquence and its truth? We may consider this central topic – the relationship between rhetoric and sincerity – by tracing it through various moments in the three volumes of Behn's fiction.

Love Letters invites the reader to empathize with protagonists who are simultaneously seen as politically reprehensible. Silvia is 'a beauty' and Philander 'our amorous hero'. One technique the epistolary mode uses to manipulate the reader into empathy with the lovers (while condemning Philander's political behaviour) is the use of dual address. In novels, letters have two addressees, the recipient and the reader. They are sent 'for' or 'to' – from Philander to 'my *Silvia*', 'adorable Silvia', 'My soul's eternal joy'. But, of course, they are primarily designed to fuel the reader's speculations and curiosity, and are, in another sense, 'for' (if not officially addressed 'to') the reader.

The three-way reader-text relations implied by epistolary fiction are illustrated by a sentence in *Love-Letters from a Nun to a Cavalier* (1678, translated by Roger l'Estrange), a text which may have influenced Behn's *Love Letters*.[8] The text ends when the nun calls a halt to writing, concluding a letter to her beloved with the phrase: 'for what necessity is there that I must be telling of you at every turn how my pulse beats?' (Todd, iv. 84, 95). 'Of' is the crucial word here, as it both suggests that the writer is telling 'of' herself to her lover and telling 'of' their relationship to the reader. In this startling use of 'of' rather than the expected 'to' we are reminded that letters, once printed, and indeed for a third party, telling 'of' events rather than being simply 'to' the named recipient.

Such a moment, in which the presence of the reader, rather than recipient, is perhaps acknowledged by the letter-text, is unusual. But the ambiguous 'telling of you' illuminates the interpretative problematic facing the reader of an epistolary novel: at the same time as the lovers are attempting to guess one another's thoughts, the text, in a larger sense, is also manipulating the reader: the letters telling things 'to' lovers and concealing them 'from' lovers are also the figures told 'of' to the spying reader. Even when Philander writes as a postscript 'I die with impatience, either to see or hear from you' we, the readers, are drawing our own conclusions.

The interpretative triangle of teller, recipient, and reader is important in *Love Letters*, particularly in the early epistolary section. This first, fully epistolary, part of the novel takes us straight into the feelings of the two lovers, obscuring as best they can the incestuous aspect of the courtship.

To Silvia.

Though I parted from you resolv'd to obey your impossible commands, yet know, oh charming *Silvia*! that after a Thousand conflicts between Love and Honour, I found the God (too mighty for the Idol) reign absolute Monarch of my Soul, and soon banished that Tyrant thence. That cruel Counsellor that would suggest to you a Thousand fond Arguments to hinder my noble pursuit; *Silvia* came in view! her irresistible *Idea*! With all the charms of blooming youth, with all the Attractions of Heavenly Beauty! Loose, wanton, gay...

(Todd, iv. 3)

This seems sincere enough. Why should either addressee or reader question these words? At first reading it seems to present a lover struggling with his feelings even though it does also seem a rather tangled and off-putting opening to a fiction. The tangle comes from the tricks Philander's language is playing. First he counterposes 'love' and 'honour'. But he values love 'the god' more highly than honour, here described as an 'idol', soon seen as a 'tyrant' and 'cruell counsellor' and, therefore, 'banished', while 'love' is quickly recuperated as 'noble'.

To a politically alert reader – as Behn's first readers were – the linking of honour with tyranny and cruelty would signal Philander's political persuasions. Any reader might notice the false logic; but one familiar with the debates counterposing love and honour would be shocked by Philander's facile resolution of a problem which was usually posed as irresolvable by human art, whether in English tragicomedy or European tragedy such as the *Cid*. And a demanding reader might find the very posing of the dilemma in terms of love and honour rather clichéd. These are all issues to which the narrative returns: but, for the present, whatever we think of Philander's rhetoric and argument, there is no reason to doubt his sincerity.

At first, then, the letters permit the reader to identify with the desires of the lovers, despite the incest. Certainly, we have direct access only to what they write, and this means that initially we see them as they present themselves to each other. Like Silvia, the reader is saturated by the lover's clichés. 'Your beauty like itself, should produce wondrous effects,' 'I have sent you the sense and truth of my soul,' 'please, give me leave (a man condemned eternally to love) to plead a little for my life', writes Philander, all too persuasively for both Silvia and the reader. Moreover, the semi-pastoral setting of Bellefont (where Silvia is confined with her parents while Philander lurks in a servant's cottage at the bottom of the garden) colludes with his rhetoric to normalize the amorous discourse.

Their romantic, even pastoral language opens the text by drawing the reader into identification with their desires. We are treated to Philander's 'restless torments...not even by the languisher himself to be expressed'. Above all, the epistolary structure plunges the reader into the relationship of the two figures without offering a third perspective which would enable us to develop a more critical understanding of Philander's charming eloquence. He writes of 'a thousand conflicts between love and honour', and rather than having the lovers' reprehensible antics displayed before us as a register of the political decay of Monmouth and his allies, the illusion of presence in the first-person epistolary narration soaks up most of the space for the reader's doubt.

However, things change as the seduction proceeds and Philander moves gradually closer to Silvia's bed. One of the first disturbing signs is that in preparation for the night of illicit bliss she has decorated her chamber and bed with flowers 'like the preparations for the dear joy of the Nuptial Bed' (Todd, iv. 43). Even a contemporary reader who had not noticed the problematic equation Philander made between monarchy and tyranny and therefore failed to pick up the subsequent irony about her preparations would surely be led to doubt the heroic status of the romance by Philander's own description of their first night of bliss:

> having overcome all difficulties, all the fatigues and trials of Love's long Sieges, Vanquish'd the mighty Fantôm of the fair, the Giant Honour, and routed all the numerous Hosts of Women's little Reasonings, passed all the bounds of peevish Modesty; Nay, even the loose and silken Counterscarps that fenced the sacred Fort, and nothing stopped my glorious pursuit: then, then, ye Gods, by an over transport, to fall just before the surrendering Gates, unable to receive the yielding treasure.

> (Todd, iv. 56)

Philander is impotent. He begs to be considered as having failed through 'excess of passion', lamenting his 'mortal killing agony, unlucky disappointment, unnatural impotence'. But Philander's sexual promiscuity – and therefore his potential to be politically unfaithful – is also suggested in his letter: 'Where shall I hide my head when this lewd story's told? . . . *Philander*, who never failed a Woman he scarce wisht for, never baulk'd the Amorous conceated Old, nor the ill-favour'd Young' (Todd, iv. 57). And what are we to make of the passivity of 'receive' and 'yielding'?

Certainly, at this point the reader begins to suspect that he is no true lover. The quasi-pastoral courtship is disturbed by Philander's libertine understanding of sexual pleasure and the failure of actions to match eloquence; and the reader is offered the opportunity of some ironic distance, a shift from sympathy to satire. The romance discourse written by Philander, and, it had seemed, the text itself, are disrupted; and the reader's empathy continues to be undermined from within the lovers' language, with their own words encouraging both empathy with them and disidentification from them. We are moved by Philander's eloquence, but then the text begins to teach us to distrust it: is he truly 'most wretched', or a libertine seducer?

The potentially problematic aspects of his very first letter, its lack of logic and clichéd way of posing the problem of illicit desire, are explored and their meanings implicitly exposed in the second volume of the story, set after the lovers have fled from France to Holland. This section of the story contrasts the faithless Silvia and Philander with the two loyal lovers, Octavio and his sister, Calista. Philander runs away from Silvia, leaving her with Octavio, and writes to her care of him. While he is away, supposedly in hiding, he sees Calista; and without realizing that she is Octavio's sister, he lays siege to her virtue and seduces her away from her aged husband. Furthermore, he then writes letters to Octavio describing the seduction and puts into the same packet other letters to be delivered to Silvia in which he maintains his love for her.

'Dear Octavio, I have sent you a Novel instead of a Letter', writes Philander (Todd, iv. 242). He describes his declaration to Calista:

> Philander to Octavio.
> I kneeling down in an humble posture, cry'd – 'Wonder not, oh Sacred Charmer of my Soul...for I am a Humble mortal that Adores you; I have a thousand Wounds, a thousand pains that prove me flesh and Blood, if you will hear my story; Oh give me leave to approach you with that Awe you do the sacred Altars; for my Devotion is as pure as that which from your Charming Lips ascends the Heavens –' With such Cant and stuff as this, which Lovers serve themselves with on occasion, I lessened the terrors of the frighted Beauty.
>
> (Todd, iv. 235–6)

This exposes as fully instrumental and insincere the very seducer's rhetoric with which we were invited to empathize in the early part of volume I. As soon as Calista does 'hear his story', his manipulative and seductive rhetoric transforms his pretend 'wounds' from love into hers, *her* ruined life and honour; his 'humble posture' is exposed as a posture indeed. In recounting his exploits to Octavio, Philander calls attention to the fact that he uses figures derived from classical, romance, and biblical narrative (the rape of Lucretia, dragons and maidens enclosed in invisible trees, the garden of Eden) – what he calls 'cant' – in order to bend Calista to his desires. The clichéd language of seduction is here seen as deployed entirely deliberately by Philander – it is no indication of his sincerity, merely a way to persuade Calista to agree to his desires. So, rather than reading lovers' language as an index of the soul (in Philander's words 'the sense and truth of my soul'), the reader begins to see it as manipulating its listener. Calista and Silvia are seduced by a rhetoric organized for this purpose – it is the receiver, not the sender, who is vulnerable to language and able to be taken in by it. And this, of course, includes that other recipient, the reader.

As the story progresses in volumes II and III, the appearance of sincerity combined with continuous shape-shifting turns out to be crucial to the survival of both Philander and Silvia, as our hero and heroine of volume I come to live by transforming themselves and preying on others. Silvia becomes as much a rhetorician and manipulator of amorous discourses as Philander, but as she does so the letters become interwoven with the words of a narrator, who comes to assume a relatively important place in the text and gives us access to the plans behind the apparently transparent meaning of her letters.

As the letters turn out to be 'false', the reader can no longer believe them: they can give us pleasure, even move us, but we are bound to have become very sceptical. Silvia's language and disguises appear to us as seductive, charming, manipulative. No longer deceived ourselves, we now have the rather different pleasure of reading letters which attempt to manipulate others. It could be said that over two volumes the reader has changed places; from being in the position of one seduced by the rhetoric of love, we have been trained to understand the position of the manipulator and seducer. By the third book we have learned to distrust not only the endearments and eternities of lovers' rhetoric but also the political ambitions of Monmouth's supporters, which the narrator indicates are entirely self-interested.

In the last volume the instrumental deployment of image and rhetoric become Silvia's means of economic survival and sexual gratification. She is in league with Philander's 'creature', Brilliard, whom she married at first to keep herself from the clutches of her parents. And 'though she was very much disordered at the apprehension of what she had suffered from a man of his character', yet 'he used the kind authority of a husband'. She lives by her body and in the third part of the novel she self-consciously assumes the status of a shape-changer. So the girl who in book I was too foolish to take clothes with her when she fled and who was taken in by Philander's rhetoric has become an adept exploiter of men. She commands the art of transformation.

In the final amour recorded by the fiction, like Miranda in *The Fair Jilt*, she has become an erotic and financial agent of her own destiny, an active sexual and economic adventurer. When she encounters the handsome libertine, Alonzo, she uses a series of *coups de théâtre* to maintain his interest, switching between men's and women's dress so that:

> she verily believed her conquest was certain; he had seen her three times, and all those times for a several Person, and yet was still in Love with her; and she doubted not, when all three were joined in one, he would be much more in love than yet he had been...
>
> *Silvia* was no sooner got home, but she resolved to receive *Alonzo* [the prospective lover], who she was assured would come: she hasted to dress herself in a very rich Suit of Man's Cloths, to receive him as the young *French* gentleman.
>
> (Todd, iv. 420)

Protean in her desires and desirability, Silvia 'is', at will, 'the young *French* gentleman', in order to reproduce the initial conditions of desire – speculation, strangeness, anticipation – and so to keep her lover to enjoy both sexually and economically. Where political and erotic power was gained by Philander's use of disguise, in so far as we are given a motivation for Silvia it is a mixture of erotic pleasuring of the self and other – a refreshing of appetite through transformation – and financial need. Economic power comes with the commodification of herself: with Brillard she 'ruined the Fortune of that young Nobleman... insomuch that... she was forced to remove for new Prey; and daily makes considerable Conquests wherever she shews the Charmer' (Todd, iv. 439). Throughout the text she is referred to as 'the charmer', or 'the fair charmer'. By book III the epithet calls attention to her role in marketing her own body, as if Silvia, separately, 'shews the Charmer' her appearance to productive erotic and financial ends, enabling her to survive on the 'Prey' of love. This transformability is similar to the quality which Angelica loses when she falls in love in *The Rover*, producing sexual and economic ruin. So shape-changing is presented as the very condition of existence; all shows are for the viewer, to manipulate the viewer as rhetoric manipulates the reader. Are there any fixed points, any relations between 'truth' and eloquence or appearance, by volume III of *Love Letters*?

A notable feature of the above passage is that it is not from a letter but from a passage of narration. The reader now knows Silvia and Philander as shape-changers and seducers, and narrative passages like this reveal what tricks of theatre and language are deployed to produce the desired effect on the person to be seduced. We must no longer listen to the seducer's rhetoric and draw our own conclusions, but are now given privy information to how Silvia's mind is really working. 'She verily believed her conquest was certain', 'she doubted not', 'she resolved to receive *Alonzo*', 'She was assured [he] would come: she hasted to dress herself' – such information allows us to know as much about Silvia as she does herself, or as a waiting-maid who has seen the whole performance.

Thus, having undermined the sincerity of first-person narrative from within, the text introduces an apparently trustworthy narrator who tells us about the mechanics of seduction. This is a subtly different kind of first-person narrator from that of *Oroonoko*. Indeed, in some ways, this first-person narrator seems to solve such interpretative problems of epistolary fiction as those posed by the triangle of teller–receiver–reader. The narrator also draws the plot back to political questions; for example, we are told that Brillard (the 'creature'–husband) will not be home until late because he is at cards with the mistress of Cesario: the seductions are taking place against a background of political intrigue.

In *Love Letters* transformability also forms a link between the political and erotic narratives. Philander, like Silvia, is a shape-changer and impersonator in the discourse of 'sincere' love; but in the sphere of politics, too, he is presented as working only for his own interest. It is hinted that he betrayed Cesario's cause to the extent that another of Cesario's followers wants to shoot him. He is not only a sexual but a political turncoat. So, although Cesario is destined by his conduct to die, the faithless Philander is able to change shape, change sides, speak a new language, and sidestep such dire consequences. He returns to the court, where, as the final summary tells us, he was 'very well understood by all good men'.

Books I and II can, in part, be read as an extended demystification of the lovers' discourse with which we were invited to empathize in the first book. These two books also, and simultaneously, use devices such as Philander's impotence and sexual and political promiscuity (and, later, his retelling of a seduction scene) to suggest the power of rhetoric. Moreover, powerful and moving rhetoric need not be connected to sexual fidelity or to political truth or nobility: it is powerful even in the wrong cause. This becomes clear to the reader, constantly moved between empathy and repugnance, as the novel unravels the deployment of rhetoric and disguise by Silvia (in sexual deceit) and Philander (in political and sexual duplicity).

But how are we to understand the voice of the first-person narrator who gradually enters the book and who helps to train us in the mistrust of rhetoric? Rather than being another voice to be doubted, it is possible to see this narrator as spying into and uncovering – discovering, to steal the theatrical term – the lies at the heart of the claims of Monmouth's rebel supporters. It is a voice which can be read as exposing Whig self-interest, pointing back to our world, outside the text, where we might be seduced by political eloquence. In doing this, of course, the politically committed narrator comes to assume the paradoxical position of one using a rhetoric of persuasion, just like the lover Philander at the opening of the novel. So, although this narrator invites our curiosity, we are not invited to take apart the workings of this particular cynical, knowing, sceptical – and apparently truthful – eloquence.

Like Behn's shorter fiction and *Oroonoko*, *Love Letters* was published at a moment when prose narrative was a diverse and marketable form. Although contemporaries enjoyed it, it was also suspect because of its power to manipulate the thoughts and feelings of the reader – the very topic which it addresses. The blurred connection between narrative and 'truth' added to both its power and its problematic status as a real-life narrative, and the first readers would have compared the accounts given by the lovers and the narrator with their own 'true' version of events.

The political aspect of *Love Letters* contrasts with many narratives of women as criminals which concentrate on the sexual nature of feminine transgression. A slightly earlier narrative than *Love Letters* is *The Case of Madam Mary Carleton* (1663), a story of the possible crime and trial of a female fraudster, probably written by Mary Carleton herself, which invited the reader's sympathy.

> Let the world now judge whether, being prompted by such plain and public signs of a design upon me, to counterplot them, I have done any more than what the rule, and a received principle of justice directs: 'to deceive the deceiver, is no deceit.'[9]

This *cause célèbre* was remembered well in Daniel Defoe's *Roxana, or the Fortunate Mistress* (1724), another text dealing with feminine agency. The subtitle brings up the question of feminine disguise and masquerade explored in *Love Letters* and *The Case of Madam Mary Carleton*, since Roxana was 'afterwards call'd the Countess of Wintselsheim, in Germany'; all these texts pose deceit and agency as bound up together. *Love Letters* differs from the two others in its publishing context and its political agenda. Crucially, where both *Roxana* and *Carleton* employed romantic, sexual, and legal discourses, and both would have been read by contemporaries as commenting on the nature and ideologies of femininity and family, *Love Letters* brings together sexual and political scandal. And, as this chapter has suggested, it characteristically educates its reader in the problems posed by eloquence in terms of both sexual and political seduction.

In *Oroonoko*, analysed in the next section, the question of the power of the narrator – in this case an equivocal one – is set alongside the power relations implicit in a slave colony. This time the power of language is mediated through the power relations between 'self' and 'other', and the question of European and other cultures.

OROONOKO: DIFFERENCE AND DOUBLENESS

> The Scene of the last Part of his [Oroonoko's] Adventures lies in a colony in *America*, called *Surinam*, in the *West-Indies*.
> But before I give you the Story of this *Gallant Slave*, 'tis fit I tell you the Manner of bringing them to these new *Colonies*; those they make Use of there, not being *Natives* of the Place; for those we live with in perfect Amity, without daring to

command 'em; but on the contrary, caress 'em with all
brotherly and friendly Affection in the World; trading with
them.... And these People represented to me an absolute
Idea of the first state of Innocence.

(Todd, iii. 57–8)

Oroonoko, or the Royal Slave is the story of the capture, enslavement,
and rebellion of Oroonoko and his beloved Imoinda. Oroonoko is
an African prince with European education, and is taken from his
home to work as a slave in the English colony of Surinam in the
1640s. There he meets up with his beloved, Imoinda. She becomes
pregnant and disaster follows.

The tale was written at the end of Behn's career, and, as this
quotation from the opening of the story suggests, while picking
up some of the issues raised in the rest of her writing, it also
makes significant new departures. These include the setting in the
colony of Surinam (which by the time of composition and
publication belonged to the Dutch), the exploration of slavery and
exoticism, and the different kinds of colonial relations of power,
trade, and ideology requiring a new slant to our analysis.

As before, the narrator has power to shape and organize events;
and the political overtones point towards the (for Behn) unwelcome
transition from James II to William and Mary. The paradox of the
royal slave – royal, yet in chains and commanded – may well hint at
Behn's views of England in 1688 when James II was a royal ruler
beset by those who did not wish to have a Roman Catholic
monarch. Such a reading would see *Oroonoko* in the light of Behn's
other fiction, particularly *Love Letters*, reworking the politics of
Stuart England in a distant location. However, while it is possible
to read into *Oroonoko* many contemporary questions of ethics and
politics, the emphasis on the specificity of 'a colony in *America*,
called *Surinam*, in the *West-Indies*' indicates the text's real interest in
the exotic and economic potential of the New World.

This text is one of the most evidently contradictory of Behn's
writings, veering between representations of Oroonoko as a
Gallant Slave, of trade, and of the innocent or dangerous natives. It
articulates (and at times comments upon) contradictions in the
relationship between Europe, the narrator, Oroonoko, slavery, and
the power to tell. Its richness stems from its instability and its
inability to hold contradictions together – the same attributes

85

which prevent it from being, as some critics have read it, an unproblematically feminist, paradigmatically abolitionist, or simply racist text.

At the end of her writing career, then, Behn was turning to new areas, especially the relationship between Europe and its 'others' which trade and slavery had made richly significant and fascinating for contemporary readers. She continues to be interested by power relations, but in this text the terms are different: set in the New World and dealing with relations between Africans and European power. Gold and sugar make Surinam significant for a late-seventeenth-century reader as a place of both exoticism and trade, and Oroonoko's double significance as a rebel slave and an educated African prince make him a paradoxical protagonist. Behn's interests in power, desire, and storytelling are reworked to focus on the questions of difference and doubleness. What does it mean for a person to be both slave and prince, European and African?

The question of whether or not Aphra Behn actually went to Surinam has been much debated. But in reading *Oroonoko* any personal experience is of less importance than the significance which Surinam had for Europeans, especially the English, and the way in which her text uses these ideas. The Europeans went to the Caribbean to look for gold. When Columbus sighted the Bahamas in 1492 he recorded: 'These islands are very green and fertile ... and it is possible that there are in them many things of which I do not know, because I did not wish to delay in finding gold'.

Initially, fantasies about the accumulation of instant wealth eclipsed all other ideas about the Caribbean. The importance of the products of the Indies are evident in the 1596 edition of Sir Walter Ralegh's account of his voyage to and encounter with Guiana, which was prefaced with an 'addition':

> Because there have beene divers opinions concieved of the gold oare brought from *Guiana*, and for that an Alderman of London and an officer of her majesties mint, hath given out that the same is of no price, I have thought by the addition of these lines to give answere as well to the said malicious slander, as to other objections.[10]

As the doubt about the value of the gold suggests, Guiana occupied an ambivalent place in European eyes. Ralegh attempted, by his insistence, to stabilize the value of Caribbean gold; and this is a major theme in a text which also details what people, vegetation, minerals, and other wonders are to be found in Guiana. Although it was not absolutely the only thing which interested travellers from Europe once they arrived, gold was the leitmotif of sixteenth-century accounts of the South American mainland, and the dominant motive for raids and contact with the native population. It was obtained by the competing Spanish, French, and English both by trade with native peoples and by setting up mines in which native labour was cruelly exploited. The rights to the mines were disputed amongst the Europeans, who would raid one another's foot- and sea-convoys transporting gold back to Europe.

Its value on the European market, combined with the far-distant places where it was found and the variously gruelling ways it was obtained, meant that gold was a commodity which, at the end of the sixteenth and beginning of the seventeenth centuries, had a confused representational value. To obtain gold, at an individual level, was to obtain a commodity which was better than money, in that it was not subject to fluctuations, and therefore it gave the owner not only wealth but also the power to control transactions. Gold was virtually magical, because it was both a medium of exchange and an object of exchange.

At the political level, then, gold was crucial to relations between the increasingly capitalistic economies of Europe. As Ralegh put it in the same address to the reader, 'it indaungereth and disturbeth all the nations of Europe, it purchaseth intelligence, creepeth into Councels, and setteth bound loyaltie at liberty in the greatest Monarchies of Europe'. Gold, as Ralegh saw it, disrupted and therefore transformed old relationships whereby a man would owe loyalty to the crown. It buys 'intelligence', useful and secret information; and it 'setteth bound loyalty at libertie', a phrase which for contemporaries would suggest not so much liberation from bonds as the tearing apart of old and formerly trusted social structures.

The cultural value of gold meant that the West Indies and South America were not peripheral in European psychic and political life in the sixteenth and seventeenth centuries, but were the focus of fantasies about wealth and difference. This is made evident in literary texts such as the poems of Camoens, John Donne, and

Andrew Marvell, and plays such as Ben Jonson's *Volpone* and *The Alchemist*. It persisted throughout the Stuart period to the renewed interest in the West Indies and Guiana during Oliver Cromwell's Protectorate (1653–8), the period in which *Oroonoko* is set, and it found new impetus in the period of colonial expansion after the Restoration of Charles II.

Gold brought the West Indies to the attention of Europe; and by the Restoration period it had acquired a more diverse economy, as colonization brought the establishment of plantations.[11] This settlement spawned a literature of its own which included travel writing and prospectuses advertising life on the plantations, organized by entrepreneurs like the Lord Governor, Francis Willoughby (a shadowy presence in Behn's narrative). The accounts bring together descriptions of new and wonderful places for the delight of the English reader at home, and information which could be used instrumentally and economically; purchasers of this literature might want to read about extraordinary places, or they might be considering going there to settle. This spectrum of interests – from exoticism to economic utility – was reflected in descriptions of Guiana and Surinam.

For example, 'The Description of Guyana' predates *Oroonoko*. It offers information on the Indians – 'Guiana hath been time out of mind ye station of ye Carrebs, and all Indians on the Island owe their originall from there' – on diseases, and on the progress of the repeated setting-up of colonies. It also gives information on commodities: 'Gold, Silver, Annetta (a Dye), Rich Gumms, Balsoms, Honey, wax, Specklewood, Fustick, Many Phisickall Druggs, Sugar Cotton & Rice'.[12] An image is produced of a dual economy: the arch-commodity gold offers one way of life, but plantation and export offer another. It was plantations which Francis Willoughby emphasized in his prospectus for Surinam, promising each single person who went 50 acres, another 50 for a wife and 30 for servants. He was keen, too, to establish community as well as economic units and especially encouraged 'able preachers, schoolmasters, Phystians, Chyrugions, midwives, Surveyors, Architectors, Chymists'.[13] George Warren's *A Full and Impartial Description of Surinam*, which some critics have regarded as the main text used by Behn in her fiction about the province, touches on nature and commodities ('sugar, speckle-wood, Cotton, Tobacco, Indico, Gums and Dying-woods'), and also on

sexuality, labour, the Indians, plantations, and the negro work-
force. In *A Publication of Guiana's Plantation* we find the Indians
regarded as a gullible source of labour because of their over-
valuation (in European terms) of payment. They will 'worke a
month or more for an axe of eighteene or twentie pence price'.[14]

  These were the dominant ways in which Surinam had been
written about, and I have quoted at length from such descriptions
because they are worth comparing with Behn's own descriptions
of wildlife and commodities, and above all her presentation of the
relations between slaves and planters. The place of Amerindians
in relation to planters was crucial to how a text would represent
the colony, with texts shifting between the emergent discourse of
the noble savage and the dangerous and devil-worshipping
'caribee'. However, in Surinam, as in much of the West Indies by
the 1600s, the slave trade was well under way. The West Indies
was part of the triangular voyages of the English merchant ships
which sailed to Africa, brought Africans as slaves to the
Caribbean, and took sugar back to England. Surinam, like other
colonies, was central to English trade and representation. In
Willoughby's prospectus from the 1650s, when *Oroonoko* is set, he
offers 'servants, English or Negroes' (Todd, iii. 177).

  Economic productivity was fused with a view of the new
continent as exotic. For example, Francis Willoughby was
involved as an entrepreneur, but also as a collector, taking
'new' objects back to Europe. In the 1650s an agent, Thomas
Povey, wrote to Willoughby 'Concerning Pressents from Suranam', 'things of price and value', to be set out in 'a Cabinett of yor
own', or 'that any of my Ladys shall entertaine themselves in
furnishing a Closett'.[15] This form of representation of the New
World was common from the first quarter of the seventeenth
century onwards, when travellers might stock a display box, or,
like John Evelyn, give over a closet to the display of a range of
curiosities. Obviously, the items in such a closet are both
'valuable' and empirical evidence of cultural difference. The
attraction of the New World and its objects is exotic and economic.
Such a combination of interests was also, of course, contradictory
in many ways: the exploitation of slaves and Indians for economic
ends did not always sit comfortably alongside a fascination with
the glamorous and exotic. As I shall suggest, these are the issues
which Behn's text addresses.

By the time *Oroonoko, or the Royal Slave* came to be published, the relatively small colony of Surinam itself, at the edge of the trade in gold and a centre of the emerging plantation economy, had generated collections and descriptions of wonders and natural vegetation as well as economic wealth. *Oroonoko* joins the writings on Surinam as a text using the twinned discourses of exoticism and romance together with economics and travel narrative. Indeed, the same uneasy social hierarchy is described in Behn's texts of the governor, planters, other Europeans, native peoples, and slaves. Like other texts, hers includes descriptions of natural wonders, the slave trade, government, economy, and wild and wonderful animals ('little *Rarities*; as *Marmosets* ... *Cousheries* ... little *Paraketoes*, great *Parrots*, *Muckaws'*). But it differs from them in that all this is framed within a narrative which threatens the delicately preserved hierarchy of the colony – the story of the life and violent death of Oroonoko who, though an African slave brought from the Cormantien coast (now Nigeria) to work on the plantations of Surinam, is royal too. He is both exotic and economic, both familiar and different; and these oppositions are inscribed on his body.

Surinam, then, is no mere backdrop in *Oroonoko*. It is part of a process whereby the difference between Europe and those places, the West Indies and Americas, viewed as sources of wealth, were themselves used to produce pleasure and fantasy for the English reader. While the exoticism of Surinam was undoubtedly economically and erotically exciting, it was also threatening in its very difference and unintelligibility; although the native Indians can be exploited by a European economy, their failure or refusal to comprehend it is also an indication of significant cultural difference, reinforced by their different colour, dress, and social and religious practices.

The potentially contradictory discourses of the economic and the exotic in relation to Surinam is echoed by other contradictions throughout the narrative. Importantly, it investigates doubleness in terms of similarity and difference – how *can* the borders between 'self' and 'other' be drawn and in any significant way maintained? – as well as through a series of narrative ambivalences both in the presentation of Oroonoko as prince and slave and in its double relation to the genres of history and romance.

The contradictions of Surinam as a site of colonial plantation economy, a location for finding gold, and an exotic destination, are worked out in the text through Oroonoko, who embodies these oppositions, and the role of the narrator. The text opens with a discussion about what kind of story it might be. Is it history (implying veracity and usefulness to the reader) or romance (broadly suggesting improbability, psychological interest)? It first claims itself as history. In the 'Dedication' we are told:

> This is a true story...if there be anything that seems romantick I beseech your Lordship to consider these countries do in all things, so far differ from ours that they produce unconceivable wonders, at least, so they appear to us because new and strange.
>
> (Todd, iii. 56)

Of course as we read on and encounter the embedded narrative of the African courtship of Imoinda and Oroonoko rendered in a combination of romantic and orientalist mode, we come to doubt the text's claims to history.

As Michael McKeon has argued, we should not underestimate the extent to which romance comes to inhabit the novel itself and the way in which both romance and history continue to be produced. McKeon suggests that we should consider how producers and consumers 'construe the relationship between "fact" and "fiction", between "history" and "literature"',[16] and this is a question posed for a reader in *Oroonoko*'s multiple styles. Certainly, sections of the text are written in different ways: we can compare, for example, the style of the narrative of the courtship of Oroonoko and Imoinda (which seems like romance) with the passages set in Surinam.

For all the romance, the narrative's claims to truth are important. As well as being associated with the genre of the novel, such 'truth–claims' are also associated with travellers' tales, situated on the border of fact and fiction. In pleasurably commodifying foreign places, such tales as *Oroonoko* both claimed to give a true account of them and played with the borders of history and romance, fact and fantasy. As William Winstanley points out, there are commercial implications in the rendering of travel into narrative designed to give pleasure to the reader: 'They that travel to view Curiosities pay dearly for their experience, but they that read Histories enjoy the Experience of all that lived before, which is far greater and much cheaper.' Truth, producing prudence, contrasts with romance: '[S]ome I have known (otherwise ingenious enough) apt to believe idle Romances, and Poetical fictions, for Historical Varieties... who will believe no otherwise but they are true.'[17]

While Winstanley wants to maintain the truth-claims of his travellers' tales, *Oroonoko* moves between acknowledging elements of romance and claiming historical veracity. Thus the reader has the double pleasure of the probable – which might be turned to economic ends – together with the thrill of the improbable and exotic. And this generic paradox is reproduced at an ideological level. The very title is contradictory; Oroonoko is presented to us in paradoxical terms, signifying both the strangeness of his situation and his own inherent strangeness, his antithetical relationship to the culture in which he finds himself.

When we first encounter Oroonoko, however, he is presented as a perfect man:

> I have often seen and conversed with this Great Man, and been a witness to many of his mighty Actions; and do assure my Reader, the most illustrious Courts could not have produced a braver Man.
>
> (Todd, iii. 6)

So the narrator introduces her own role and the central figure. She declares that everything in the story has been told to her either by the protagonist himself or by an eyewitness, and outlines Oroonoko's life from his courtship of Imoinda in Africa to his rebellion against slavery in Surinam. So the story has many elements to give pleasure to a European reader: first, told in an embedded narrative, the innocent courtship between Oroonoko and Imoinda is troubled by the jealous desires of Oroonoko's grandfather, another of Behn's lascivious but impotent old men 'now grown to his second Childhood'. 'Contrary to the custom of his Country', Oroonoko makes Imoinda a vow 'she should be the only woman he would possess while he liv'd; that no Age or Wrinkles should incline him to change' (Todd, iii. 65), and sticks to these vows although his aged relative intervenes and sells her into slavery. Then Oroonoko himself is ensnared into slavery by the false vows of the sea captain, and delivered to the colony of Surinam.

Surinam was under English rule in the 1640s, when the story is set, but had been taken by the Dutch by the time Behn's narrative was published. In Surinam Oroonoko, by coincidence, is reintroduced to Imoinda, who is the object of the rapacious desires of the white plantation owners. Although, as slaves, they are purchased and renamed, they are also proposed by the narrator as man and wife. When Imoinda becomes pregnant, the fact that their child will be born into slavery exposes their good treatment as a privilege. For their wedding 'there was as much magnificence as the country could afford'. Yet the narrator tells us that Oroonoko suspected that, although he offered 'either gold, or a vast quantity of slaves' as payment for his liberty – for he is presented throughout as happy to trade in slaves – his captors will ensure that his child is born into slavery.

Imoinda's pregnancy introduces the question of the reproduction of social conditions through biological reproduction, and precipitates a turning-point in the text as the interests of Oroonoko and his masters diverge dramatically and the story becomes increasingly ambivalent, the narrator offering no comment, for example, on Oroonoko's mistrust of his masters. This ambivalence increases when the 'heroic' Oroonoko organizes a revolt of the slaves rather than have his princely child reared as one. Although his motivations suggest Behn's familiar interest in the proper integration of actual status and natural nobility, the narrator's distance from events troubles any understanding of the text as sympathetic to slave revolt in general. And from this point the paradox of Oroonoko's different and ambivalent status – as royal and slave, educated noble and rebel, European and African, reader's erotic object and dangerous other, economic unit and tale-teller – becomes increasingly disturbing, leading to the shocking denouement.

The particular aspect of doubleness situated by the text as 'in' Oroonoko but potentially highly disruptive to the delicate social fabric of already quarrelsome Surinam society is reiterated and highlighted once Oroonoko has been brought to Surinam and is named as a slave. Where Imoinda is given the name Clemene, associated with romance, Oroonoko is renamed Caesar; and the text makes much of the Roman associations of the name as an index of Caesar's nobility. Thus each of the royal and enslaved pair have, appropriately, two names: one European and one African.

The power of the narrator to describe in paradoxical ways, and therefore invite a doubleness in our response, is clear throughout.

93

For example, she invites our ambivalence about cultural difference when she describes the innocent first courtship of Oroonoko and Imoinda. Imoinda is naked; and the narrator comments, 'Where there is no Novelty, there can be no Curiosity.' More importantly, when Oroonoko himself appears, the narrator gives us a very detailed description of him:

> He was pretty tall, but of a Shape the most exact that can be fansy'd: The most Famous Statuary co'd not form the Figure of a Man more admirably turn'd from Head to Foot. His Face was not of that brown, rusty Black which most of that Nation are, but a perfect Ebony, or polish'd Jett. His Eyes were the most awful that cou'd be seen, and very piercing; the *White* of 'em being like Snow, as were his Teeth. His Nose was rising and Roman, instead of *African* and flat. His Mouth, the finest shap'd that cou'd be seen; far from those great turn'd Lips which are so natural to the rest of the *Negroes*.

(Todd, iii. 62–3)

In a scene which is repeated with variations in *Robinson Crusoe* and elsewhere, the text inverts the reader's assumptions about the differences between African and European physiognomy, both of which are used in a description of one figure. Each detail of Oroonoko's face which might have been expected to betray his African nature – shape, colour, nose, lips – are coded as not what would be expected, but as its European opposite. However, such a passage relies on the reader's assumptions not only about what an African face looks like but also that an African physique is inferior. Thus the text assumes that, usually, an African would not be 'admirably turn'd', like the men of Greek statuary, would not be white but 'rusty' (itself a word suggesting decay), and so on. As a physical being, therefore, Oroonoko is present in the text twice: once as the African that the European reader might expect to see, and once as the ideal of masculine beauty in Western culture; and this mirrors his double presence as king and slave. Notably, this passage does not merge European and African characteristics, but presents them as antithetical attributes: the presence of African characteristics is not posed as blending into or compatible with European looks.

Contrastingly, the narration poses Imoinda, as Ros Ballaster notes, as different rather than, doubly, similar *and* different. She is described as richly carved, and therefore identifiable as culturally distinct; there is no scene similar to this enumeration of

Oroonoko's parts. Rather, she plays a structuring role in the narrative because of her body, first the focus of Oroonoko's desire and then the cause of the rebellion because Oroonoko does not want his child to be born into slavery. Coded as different, she does not participate in the contradictory closeness suggested by the overlayeredly African/European description of Oroonoko. When she dies, murdered by Oroonoko, the text proposes her death as a product of African rather than European custom. Yet, of course, it is the question of the physical and social reproduction of slavery through her body which precipitates the rebellion and her death.

The contradictions between the social and economic value of her maternity produce her death; but at the end of the text she reappears, closing it with a reference to the narrator's ability to make her famous as 'the brave, the beautiful and the constant *Imoinda*'. Where Oroonoko embodies contradiction, Imoinda is a constantly different subject, caught up in the contradictory ideologies of maternity and slavery: less central to the text than Oroonoko, she is part of the process of conflict between Europeans and others over the ideologies of pregnancy and slavery.

The reader thus perceives the primary relationship in the story as that between Oroonoko and the white European narrator; while Imoinda, although structurally central, is displaced from the reader's interest (and, one might say, plays less of a part in her own story), being the African and different object of Oroonoko's desire rather than the subject which creates the narrative.

The description of Oroonoko's person, on the other hand, indicates the narrator's interest in his body and positions him as a symptom of the troubled hierarchy of Surinam, appearing as it does after the text's first description of the native population. In the context of accounting for the presence of African slaves in Surinam, the narrator explains that, because the native population outnumber the Europeans, they are not used as slaves. Rather the Europeans trade with them. She goes on to describe them as dressed 'as Adam and Eve did', loving innocently, 'so like out first parents before the fall', and living as 'an absolute idea of the first state of innocence, before man knew how to sin'.

Thus, where the slaves are seen as dangerous, the native population not involved in work with Europeans are valorized as noble savages. Such an Edenic view of them echoes some contemporary writers, such as the French Jean Baptiste du Tertre, who published writings on his visit to the French West Indies, arguing, 'In truth our Savages are Savages in name only...For they are just as nature brought them forth, that is to say, with great simplicity and natural naivety.'[18] George Warren in his *Description* refers to the good qualities of the Indians, but also condemns the slave trade by which Africans are 'brought out of Guiny in Africa to those parts, where they are sold like *Dogs,* and no better esteem'd but for their Work sake' (Todd, iii. 19). As in the narration of *Oroonoko,* a further complexity is introduced by the interrelationships between the Europeans, slaves, and the native population.

Oroonoko puts the slaves, and more particularly Oroonoko himself, into contrast with the Indians in terms of economics, appearance, and habits: the native population is associated with distinct social practices, with the distant rural part of the river, and with the gold economy. On a trip up the river with Oroonoko the narrator reports: 'We met with some Indians of strange aspect...and brought along with 'em bags of gold dust...We carry'd these men up to Parham, where they were kept till the Lord Governour came.' The contrast between Oroonoko and the native population is maintained throughout the text, and when he and the narrator go upriver to visit an Indian settlement, his presence is contrasted with that of an interpreter whom the text describes, contradictorily, as a European fisherman so bronzed by the sun as to be 'a perfect Indian in colour'. The fisherman–interpreter assumes a position something like the beachcomber-figure of nineteenth-century literature, living between the two groups, Indians and Europeans. He has respect for each (in this text witnessed by his unwillingness to go up the river), trades with each, but remains, because of his very position on the threshold, a figure of some ambiguity and, potentially, an object of distrust.

Oroonoko, though he too mediates between Indians and Europeans, never becomes such a blurred or blended threshold figure. Rather, he is maintained by the text as a living contradiction. This is posed for the reader as an increasingly acute problem towards the end of the narrative, at the point of the slave rebellion and after. It is as if, like the society Oroonoko is presented as rebelling against in Surinam, the narrator and even the text have no way of accepting or disarming the danger inherent in their own contradictions – and this becomes apparent in the final section of the narrative.

While the Indians and the slaves are two clearly distinct groups, the narration is not fully clear about the relationship between Oroonoko and slavery. On the one hand, he is distinguished from the slaves, who are 'base' where he is 'royal'; on the other, he becomes their leader. We are told that he 'made an harangue to 'em on the miseries and ignomies of slavery'. And, after the slaves have escaped, the narrator gives an ambivalent account of the pursuit. Thus the issue of slave labour in itself tends to be sublimated in the narrator's relationship with Oroonoko and the posing of his actions as individual rather than social. In their part in the rebellion the slaves are distinguished from Oroonoko in their lack of fortitude; despite their response to his rhetoric of freedom, they abandon the struggle.

Thus, from being fêted as a wonder, albeit an isolated figure made up of paradoxes, at the level of story Oroonoko becomes literally isolated, alone, outside the (European) camps, distant from the slaves, and utterly different from the native population. When found by the search party sent out after the rebellion, Oroonoko is in the wilderness, alone with the corpse of the pregnant Imoinda murdered by his own hand, and too weak to kill himself. At this point Oroonoko is described as an image of death – 'so alter'd that his face was like a death's-head black'd over, nothing but teeth and eyeholes' – and this is how the story, ultimately, places him.

The contradictions are reinforced by the narrator, whose ambivalence is increasingly impressed on the reader; on the one hand, she tells us how much she admired Oroonoko and how she wished his story had been written by someone more fitted to the task. She details his learning and his past life in Africa, said to have been told to her by the hero himself, as well as giving a full description of his treatment at the hands of the villain of the piece – William Byam, the deputy governor, whom she characterizes as entirely over-reacting to the rebellion organized by Oroonoko. Moreover, she puts into Oroonoko's own mouth a long speech against slavery, and endorses his understanding of Europeans as vow-breakers. On the other hand, the narrator seems to be involved in lying to Oroonoko; she helps to feed him promises from day to day, awaiting the arrival of the Lord Governor, and she voices her mistrust and identification with the English colony:

'After this, I neither thought it convenient to trust him much out of our view, not did the country who fear'd him.' So, even as she is Oroonoko's great defender, the narrator's duplicitousness tends to contradict readers who understand this text as unproblematically abolitionist, rendering it, rather, a text of interest because of its very full articulation of contradictory positions on slavery and power relations, and laying out these contradictions for the reader.

The narrator appears to become powerless towards the end of the story, absenting herself from the scenes in which Oroonoko is condemned. She tells us that when he is brought back from the wilderness to the camp 'the earthy smell about him was so strong, that I was persuaded to leave the place for some time', and she takes a boat upriver. Because she is not there, the nature of Oroonoko's death is not posed for us as an *ethical* problem. It becomes inevitable – and is willed by him – while she is out of the way. Rather than attempting to answer, decide, or unravel the contradictions and paradoxes that the story has so energetically built up, its final moments tear them apart, as the figure of Oroonoko, assembled out of contradictions in the passages I have quoted, is textually torn apart.

In the last moments of his life, which ends as the story ends, the narrator's mother and sister stand by, sympathetic but 'not suffer'd to save him; so rude and wild were the rabble, and so inhuman were the justices who stood by to see the execution'. At the point at which the mediating ambivalence of the narrator is, notionally, removed (of course, she continues to tell the story though absent from the events), the contradictory aspects of Oroonoko are dismantled. Hot peppers are rubbed into his wounds, and he is burned and dismembered as the society of Surinam punishes him as a rebel slave. Ultimately, the society he is in finds a single and singular meaning for him – that of dead slave. But, as readers fascinated by his doubleness, we are treated to the spectacle of the text resolving it in an orgy of narrative violence which tears apart its protagonist.

> He had learn'd to take Tobacco; and when he was assur'd he should die, he desir'd they would give him a Pipe in his Mouth, ready lighted; which they did: And the Executioner came, and first cut off his Members, and threw them into the Fire; after that, with an ill-favour'd knife, they cut off his Ears and his Nose, and burned them;

he still smoak'd on, as if nothing had touch'd him; then they hack'd off one of his Arms, and still he bore up and held his Pipe, but at the cutting off of the other Arm, his head sunk, and his Pipe dropt, and he gave up the Ghost, without a Groan, or a Reproach.

(Todd, iii. 118)

Oroonoko ends with the death of its troubling protagonist. This passage, obviously, puts an end to the contradiction constituted by him which had both generated and disturbed the narrative. The incredible cruelty and violence of that end suggest both the troubling valency of the kind of contradiction represented by Oroonoko in the late-seventeenth-century culture which produced and read the text, and the text's own highly ambivalent relationship to its subject.

Notably, the final scene reworks the earlier one in which Oroonoko's contradictory beauties are named for us. The terms in which this is enacted involve a removal of that contradictory doubleness emphasized in that earlier description of his looks: the very sites described in that *blazon* of Oroonoko's body – nose, limbs, eyes – are here removed, erased, or put out, as the double figure is literally dismembered. So where narrator and reader had found stereotypes of African and European irresolubly overlayered in the description of Oroonoko's beauty, here its troubling constituent parts are separated. First his 'Members' are destroyed – this seems to indicate his genitals, and therefore reminds us of the way the whole question of freedom centred on the meaning of Oroonoko's ability to reproduce. And then, one by one, those features which refused to be either fully European or fully African – face and body – are destroyed. The activity of dismemberment, separating out a figure always posed as a paradox, offers a conclusion to the narrative in terms of the return of that paradox to its constituent parts, now dead rather than living.

However, while Oroonoko is destroyed by the narrative in terms which violently separate him into parts, the ambivalent status accorded to him as simultaneously African and European is sustained because he is stoically smoking. He is consuming one of the products of Surinam which, though not at the time produced extensively by slave labour, came to be an index of slave culture. Thus, he is reinscribed as a slave producer and consumer of European culture in terms of the pipe. As a smoker, Oroonoko is placed as subject to European culture and returned to the position of a participant in the economic significance of the West Indies to Europe – the other aspect of the exotic and fascinating, different place.

The violence of Oroonoko's dismemberment, while it moves the reader's compassion, is also structured to provide narrative closure, a grand finale in the death of the protagonist. As his body is torn apart, the narrative ends are sewn up for the reader. And the ideological contradictions foregrounded by the text's having taken an African prince and slave as its protagonist and a white Englishwoman as narrator are not so much resolved as exploded into fragments. In this troubling way, the text positions us as 'satisfied' by his death: it even fulfils an early promise from the very first page that 'the last part' of Oronooko's adventures were set in Surinam, reaffirming the narrator's control over the text. A final paradox remains: the violent death of its problematic hero, watched by the female relatives of an absent narrator, provides the reader with a disturbing closure to a troubling text.

In the narrative working-out of the fate of Oroonoko, the text poses for a reader some of the late seventeenth century's contradictory attitudes to cultural difference and slavery. In establishing the paradox of Oroonoko, the text lays bare some of the irreconcilable paradoxes of Eurocentric perceptions of difference and similarity, only to erase them. The confusions articulated through the description of Oroonoko's body are about the perfection or monstrosity of the culturally different and enslaved subject.

Oroonoko both offers ideological positions and presents a critique of them. Certainly, the juxtaposition of white female narrator and black slave has sent critics searching for a key to understand the relationship between the two. However, as I suggested in the introduction, part of the interest of Behn's texts is the way they shift between circulating cultural assumptions and offering a critique of them. Like her other fiction, this text points back to the contradictory ideologies of late-seventeenth-century England. But it locates these contradictions in a society which is fascinating for its wealth and exoticism – and which suggests the confusions of power relationships in a particularly extreme way.

5

Conclusion

This book has traced the patterns of desire, storytelling, and political analysis through a wide range of Behn's texts written throughout her career. As the Introduction suggested, Behn is in many ways a protean writer, consistently responsive not only to politics but also to market concerns, always alert to the commercial value of a text. As such, her writings require many different frames of reference.

The close attention paid to poetry, theatre, and prose has shown Behn to be generically adaptable and adroit, always responding rapidly to the challenges of a particular medium. The commercial production of the texts means not only that her writing covers a huge span, from royal panegyric to political ballad, from epilogue to tragedy, from short fiction to blockbuster *roman à clef*, but that it constantly engages with issues of interest to its public. This connection with a public sphere which was simultaneously political and commercial, using pleasure to sell (literally) political opinion produces one of the most exciting aspects of Behn's writing – a continuing and contradictory engagement with the ideologies produced by her society.

Indeed, as these short readings may have indicated, a 'Behn' text both offers a complex and pleasurable manipulation of its audience and articulates contemporary ideological positions. At moments her texts comment upon these positions. But their commercial inclusiveness means that, amongst the paradoxes, many issues and positions contradictory to dominant codes are voiced, if not endorsed. As caricatures, Commonwealthsmen and republicans not only are given a voice (albeit one framed by satire) but, set in contrast to varying sorts of royalists, provide the pleasure of the comedies. The poems suggest that feminine desire is destructive, but elsewhere suggest that it is self-originating –

always a desire to desire, and polymorphously perverse in the fantasies it creates.

Thus, Behn's texts, although introduced virtually alone here, invite comparative and contextual analysis as part of the cultural and political public sphere of late-seventeenth-century England. In *Oroonoko* we see Behn right at the end of her career blending old concerns with experimental narrative genre and narration, and taking them in a new – and, crucially, marketable – direction. As such it is a fitting conclusion to a career which invites not so much the fetishization of the author as the placing of a huge number of texts with some similarities but many differences against a range of material, cultural, political, and critical contexts. It is my contention that such a study would produce not a liberal or easily protean Behn canon, but one in which we can read the contradictions of the emergence of a post-war political literary sphere, as well, perhaps, as an occasional commentary upon the contradictions between the ideals and exigencies of economic, sexual, and political modernity.

Notes

CHAPTER 1. INTRODUCTION

1 Catherine Gallagher, 'The Networking Muse: Aphra Behn as Heroine of Frankness and Self-discovery,' *TLS* (Sept. 10, 1993), 3–4.
2 For the state of play on biography, see Janet Todd and Francis McKee, 'The "She Spy": Unpublished Letters on Aphra Behn, Secret Agent',*TLS* (10 Sept, 1993), 4–5.
3 Maureen Duffy, *The Passionate Shepherdess* (London, 1977), 11.
4 Angeline Goreau, *Reconstructing Aphra: A Social Biography of Aphra Behn* (Oxford, 1980), 3.
5 Virginia Woolf, *A Room of One's Own* (1929); ed. Morag Shiach (Oxford, 1992), 78–85.
6 Jacqueline Rose, *The Haunting of Sylvia Plath* (London, 1991), pp. xi–xiv, 1.
7 Ronald Hutton, *The Restoration* (Oxford, 1985); Robin Clifton, *The Last Popular Rebellion* (London, 1984); for a sympathetic account of the nonconformist position, see Richard L. Greaves, '"To Be Found Faithful": The Nonconformist Tradition in England 1660–1700', *Bunyan Studies*, 4 (Spring 1991), 37–65.

CHAPTER 2. POETRY

1 Todd, *Works*, I. pp. xlv–xlvi.
2 See Keith Walker, *The Poems of John Wilmot Earl of Rochester* (Oxford, 1984), p. xii; on manuscript lampoons, see W. J. Cameron, 'A Late Seventeenth-century Scriptorium', *Renaissance and Modern Studies*, 7 (1963), 25–52; Mary Ann O'Donnell, 'A Verse Miscellany of Aphra Behn: Bodleian Library Ms Firth c. 16', in *English Manuscript Studies*, 2, ed. Peter Beal and Jeremy Griffiths (Oxford, 1990), 189–230.
3 Todd, *Works*, 1, pp. xl, xli.
4 Ibid. p. xxxix.
5 *Aesop's Fables* (London, 1665), English transl. by Thomas Philipott;

Aesop's Fables (London, 1673), English poetry by Behn. See Annabel Patterson, *Fables of Power: Aesopian Writing and Political History*, (London, 1991), 85–8.

6 John Hollander, *The Figure of Echo* (Berkeley, 1981), 8. For Echo, see also 'Song: The Surprise', Todd, *Works*, i. 80.

7 *The Collected Works of Katherine Philips*, ed. Patrick Thomas (Stump Cross, 1990), 12. See also Elaine Hobby, 'Katherine Philips: Seventeenth Century Lesbian Poet', in *What Lesbians Do in Books* (London, 1991), 183–205. Behn, e.g., refers to Orinda in her transl. of Abraham Cowley's 'Of Plants, Book vi' (Todd, *Works*, i, 325, 590–4).

8 'To Orinda: An Imitation of Horace, By the Earl of Roscommon', in *The Temple of Death*, 2nd edn. (London, 1695), 55 (listed under Wharton). See Jeslyn Medoff, 'The Daughters of Behn and the Problem of Reputation', in Isobel Grundy & S. Wiseman (eds.), (London, *Women, Writing, History*, 1992), 33–54.

9 'To Mrs Behn, on what she writ of the Earl of Rochester', *The Temple of Death*, p. 242–3.

10 See Todd, i. 402, 405.

11 Keith Walker (ed.) *Poems of Rochester*, 31; George Etherege, 'The Imperfect Enjoyment', in *Temple of Death*, 180. For another reading of Behn's 'The Disappointment', see Carol Barash, 'Behn's Erotic Poetry', in *Teaching Eighteenth Century Poetry*, Christopher Fox (ed.); (New York, 1990), 166–7.

12 See Rosalind Ballaster, *Seductive Forms: Women's Amatory Fiction from 1684 to 1740* (Oxford, 1992), 75–9, 89–95.

13 Ibid. 76. Compare Ann Rosalind Jones and Peter Stallybrass, 'Fetishising Gender: Constructing the Hermaphrodite in Renaissance Europe', and Randolph Trumbach, 'London's Sapphists: From Three Sexes to Four Genders in the Making of Modern Culture', both in Julia Epstein and Kristina Straub (eds.), *Bodyguards: The Cultural Politics of Gender Ambiguity* (London, 1991), 80–111, 112–41, with Thomas Lacquer, *Making Sex* (London, 1990).

CHAPTER 3. PLAYS

1 John Dryden, 'Preface' to *An Evening's Love* (1671), repr. in *Restoration and Eighteenth Century Comedy*, ed. Scott McMillan (New York, 1973), 352. On Spanish influence, see John Loftis, *The Spanish Plays of Neoclassical England* (New Haven and London, 1973), 56–9, 147 *et passim*. See also Laura Brown, *English Dramatic Form 1660–1760* (New Haven, 1981).

2 Thomas Hobbes, *On Human Nature* (1650), in *Restoration and Eighteenth Century Comedy*, ch. 9, 343.

3 *The Country Gentleman's Vade Mecum* (1699), quoted in Peter Holland, *The Ornament of Action* (Cambridge, 1979), 39; audience fig. 16. See also David Roberts, *The Ladies* (Oxford, 1984); and Laura J. Rosenthal, ' "Counterfeit Scrubbado": Women Actors in the Restoration', *The Eighteenth Century*, 34/1 (1993), 3–22.

4 Samuel Vincent, *The Young Gallant's Academy* (London, 1674), 55–6.

5 Mary Ann O'Donnell, 'Aphra Behn: Tory Wit and Unconventional Woman', in Katherine M. Wilson and Frank Warnke (eds.), *Women Writers of the Seventeenth Century* (London, 1989), 341–74; Holland, *Ornament*, 20–33.

6 See Nancy Cotton, *Women Playwrights in England* (Lewisburg, 1980).

7 Thomas Shadwell, 'The Tory Poets: A Satyr', in *The Complete Works of Thomas Shadwell*, ed. Montague Summers (London, 1927), iii. 275–6.

8 *Works of Mr. Thomas Brown* (repr. London, 1760), ii. 154–5. Quoted Cotton, *Women Playwrights*, 75.

9 Robert Gould, *Poems Chiefly Consisting of Satyrs and Satyrical Epistles*, (1689), 161–79. See also 'Prologue', 53.

10 That said, many people actually writing for the theatre had origins of higher social status than either Behn or Gould seem to have had.

11 For example, Cheri Davis Langdell slides from epilogues to 'heroines' to 'Aphra' when she asserts: 'The persona of the epilogue, epistles, prefaces, etc., of Aphra Behn is of course the same woman whom Behn depicts as heroine or lucky victor in her plays. Like their author, the heroines of Behn's plays engage in the sexual-political battle', ('Aphra Behn and Sexual Politics: A Dramatist's Dialogue with her Audience', in James Redmond (ed.), *Themes in Drama* (Cambridge, 1985), 109–28, 117). See also Elizabeth Schafer, 'Appropriating Aphra', *Australian Drama Studies*, 19 (Oct. 1991), 39–49.

12 Mary Ann O'Donnell, *Aphra Behn: An Annotated Bibliography* (New York, 1986), lists three plays attributed to Behn: *The Debauchee*, *The Counterfeit Bridegroom*, and *The Revenge*. Readers of Thomas Southerne's theatrical adaptation of Behn's fiction, *Oroonoko* (1695), might be interested to note that even as they reject the idea that Southerne borrowed from *The Counterfeit Bridegroom*, the editors fail to note this attribution in their introduction to Southerne's play. See *Oroonoko*, ed. Maximillian E. Novak and David Stuart Rodes (London, 1976), p. xxvi.

13 See Richard L. Greaves, *Secrets of the Kingdom: British Radicals from the Popish Plot to the Revolution of 1688–1689* (Stanford, 1992), pp. vii–x; Rev. Robert Kirk, quoted by William Van Lennep, *The London Stage 1660–1800* (Illinois, 1965), 378.

14 Robert D. Hume, *The Development of English Drama in the Late Seventeenth Century* (Oxford, 1976, repr. 1977), 340.

15 See Annabel Patterson, *Reading Between the Lines* (London, 1992), 210–13.

16 J. P. Kenyon, *The Popish Plot* (Harmondsworth, 1972, repr. 1974), 72, 96;

BL Add. MS 32059 fos. 47–8, North Papers, quoted 111.
17 See Leslie Ann Uphadyay, 'Two Political Comedies of the Restoration: John Tatham's *The Rump* and Aphra Behn's Adaptation, *The Round-heads*' (unpubl. Ph. D. thesis, Univ. of London, 1974).
18 Jonathan Scott, *Algernon Sidney and the Restoration Crisis* (Cambridge, 1991), 164–5. John Verney, May 1681, Bucks R/O M11/35; quoted in Scott, 162, from Mark Knights, 'Politics and Opinion in the Exclusion Crisis', (Oxford, D. Phil., 1989), 18; and from James II, *Original Papers*, ed. MacPherson (1775), 112.
19 Fidelis Morgan, *The Female Wits* (London, 1981), 73.
20 Holland, *Ornament*, 28–33, 41–50; Elin Diamond, '*Gestus* and Signature in Aphra Behn's *The Rover*', *English Literary History*, 56/3 (1989), 519–41.
21 Greaves, *Secrets*, 290–5; Clifton, *Last Popular Rebellion*, 232; Ford, Lord Grey of Werke, *Secret Narrative of the Rye-House Plot* (London, 1754); John Whiting, *Persecution Expos'd*, 153, quoted in Greaves, *Secrets*, 293.
22 Terry Castle, *Civilisation and Masquerade* (Stanford, 1986), 2, 4.
23 Natalie Zemon Davis, *Society and Culture in Early Modern France*, (London, 1975).
24 On the portraits of Angelica Bianca, see Elin Diamond, '*Gestus* and signature in Aphra Behn's *The Rover*', *ELH* 56/3, (Fall 1989), 519–41.
25 O'Donnell, in Wilson and Warnke (eds.), *Seventeenth Century*, 346.

CHAPTER 4. FICTION

1 Michael McKeon, *The Origins of the English Novel 1600–1740* (London, 1988); Lennard Davis, *Factual Fictions* (New York, 1983). See Jane Spencer, *The Rise of the Woman Novelist* (Oxford, 1986). My reading is indebted to Rosalind Ballaster's discussion in *Seductive Forms*, 69–114. Thanks to Helen Hackett for putting Behn's short fiction in the context of romance.
2 Peter Brooks, *Reading for the Plot* (London, 1992).
3 Vladimir Propp, *The Morphology of the Russian Folktale* (Austin, Tex., 1968), 53–5, 67.
4 Ross Chambers, *Story and Situation* (Minneapolis, 1984), 3.
5 References are to *Love Letters between a Nobleman and his Sister (1684–7)*, ed. Janet Todd (London, 1995).
6 Ian Watt, *The Rise of the Novel* (1957), repr. 1987), 10: e.g. McKeon, *Origins*, 25–7.
7 Rosalind Ballaster, *Seductive Forms*, 86.
8 *Five Love Letters from a Nun to a Cavalier*, trans. Roger l'Estrange (London, 1678), B4^v. See also Peggy Kamuf, *Discourses of Feminine Desire* (Lincoln, Neb., 1982).

9 *The Case of Madam Mary Carleton* (1663), see also Graham, Hinds, *et al.*, *Her Own Life* (London, 1990), 135; Hero Chalmers, ' "The Person I Am, or What they Made Me to Be" ', in Brandt and Purkiss (eds.), *Women, Texts and Histories*, 164–94.

10 Columbus, *Journal*, quoted by Peter Hulme, *Colonial Encounters* (London, 1986), 23; Sir Walter Ralegh, *The Discoveries of . . . Guiana* (London, 1656), 'To the Readers', q2^r. BL C. 32. c. 10. See Rosalind Ballaster, 'The New Hystericism: Aphra Behn's *Oroonoko*: The Body, the Text and the Feminist Critic', in Isobel Armstrong (ed.)., *New Feminist Discourses* (London, 1992), 283–95.

11 J. L. Lorimer, *English and Irish Settlement on the River Amazon* (London, 1989), 2nd ser., 171; J. A. Williamson, *English Colonies in Guiana and the Amazon, 1604–1668* (Oxford, 1923).

12 'The Description of Guyana', in *Colonising Expeditions to the West Indies and Guiana 1623–1677* (London, 1925), lvi. 134-5.

13 'Certaine Overtures Made by Ye Lord Willoughby of Parham unto all such as shall incline to plant in ye colony of Suranam on ye continent of Guiana' (London, 1656, 174–7.) See also Egerton MSS 2395 fos. 279–82.

14 George Warren, *A Full and Impartial Description of Surnam* (London, 1667), 2–24; Earl of Berkshire, *A Publication of Guiana's Plantation* (London, 1632), 15. 1061. g. 13.

15 BL Add. MS 11411, Thomas Povey, 'Booke of Entrie of Forreigne Letters: 1655: 1656: 1657: 1658: 1659: 1660', f14^v.

16 Michael McKeon, *The Origins of the English Novel 1600–1740* (London, 1988), 28.

17 William Winstanley *Histories and Observations Domestick and Foreign* (London, 1683), A5$^{r–v}$.

18 Jean Baptiste du Tertre (1667), quoted in transl. from *Wild Majesty: Encounters with Caribs From Columbus to the Present Day. An Anthology*, ed. Peter Hulme and Neil L. Whitehead (Oxford, 1992), 128–9.

Select Bibliography

WORKS BY APHRA BEHN

At present texts of Behn's writings are in transition. This study has made use of Janet Todd's edition of the *Works* where available, using Summers when Todd was unavailable. Therefore, quotations from plays still refer to the Summers edition. Many selections of Behn's texts and scholarly editions of single texts are now available: I have not listed these.

Editions

The Works of Aphra Behn, ed. Montague Summers, vols. i–vi (London, 1915).
The Works of Aphra Behn, ed. Janet Todd, vols. i–iv (London, 1992–5).

BIBLIOGRAPHY

O'Donnell, Mary Ann, *Aphra Behn: An Annotated Bibliography of Primary and Secondary Sources* (New York, 1986).

CRITICAL STUDIES

Monographs, collections, biographies

Duffy, Maureen, *The Passionate Shepherdess* (London, 1977).
Goreau, Angeline, *Reconstructing Aphra: A Social Biography of Aphra Behn* (Oxford, 1980).
Hutner, Heidi (ed.), *Rereading Aphra Behn: History, Theory, Criticism* (Charlottesville, Va., 1993).
Sackville-West, Vita, *Aphra Behn: The Incomparable Astrea* (London, 1927).
Todd, Janet (ed.), *Aphra Behn Studies* (Cambridge, 1996).
—— *The Secret Life of Aphra Behn* (London, 1996).

Woodcock, George, *The Incomparable Aphra* (London, 1948).

Poetry

Barash, Carol, 'Behn's Erotic Poetry', in Christopher Fox (ed.), *Teaching Eighteenth Century Poetry* (New York, 1990).

Lilley, Kate, 'Blazing Worlds: Seventeenth-Century Women's Utopian Writing', in Claire Brandt and Diane Purkiss (eds.), *Women, Texts & Histories* (London, 1992).

Medoff, Jeslyn, 'The Daughters of Behn and the Problem of Reputation', in Isobel Grundy and S. Wiseman (eds.), *Women, Writing, History* (London, 1992).

Merman, Dorothy, 'Women Becoming Poets: Katherine Philips, Aphra Behn, Anne Finch', *English Literary History*, 57 (1990), 335–55.

Patterson, Annabel, *Fables of Power* (London, 1991).

Drama

Brown, Laura, *English Dramatic Form 1660–1760* (New Haven, 1981).

Carlson, Susan, 'Aphra Behn and the Possibilities of a Countertradition', in *Women and Comedy: Rewriting the British Theatrical Tradition* (Michigan, 1991).

Copeland, Nancy, '"Once a whore and ever"? Whore and Virgin in *The Rover* and its Antecedents', *Restoration*, 16/1 (Spring 1992), 20–7.

Cotton, Nancy, *Women Playwrights in England. c.1363–1750* (East Brunswick, NJ, 1980).

Diamond, Elin, '*Gestus* and Signature in Aphra Behn's *The Rover*', *English Literary History*, 56 (1989), 519–41.

Gallagher, Catherine, 'Who was that Masked Woman? The Prostitute and the Playwright in the Comedies of Aphra Behn', *Women's Studies*, 15, (1988), 23–42.

Hendricks, Margo, 'Civility, Barbarism, and Aphra Behn's *The Widow Ranter*', in Margo Hendricks and Patricia Parker (eds.), *Women, 'Race', and Writing* (London, 1994).

Owen, Susan J., '"Suspect my loyalty when I lose my virtue": Sexual Politics and Party in Aphra Behn's Plays of the Exclusion Crisis', *Restoration*, 18/1 (Spring 1994), 37–47.

Patterson, Annabel, 'The Good Old Cause', in *Reading Between the Lines* (London, 1993).

Fiction

Armstrong, Nancy, *Desire and Domestic Fiction* (Oxford, 1987).

Ballaster, Rosalind, 'New Hystericism: Aphra Behn's *Oroonoko*: The Body, the Text and the Feminist Critic', in Isobel Armstrong (ed.), *New Feminist Discourses* (London, 1992).

—— 'Siezing the means of Seduction: Fiction and Feminine Identity in Aphra Behn and Delarivier Manley', in Isobel Grundy and S. Wiseman (eds.), *Women, Writing, History* (London, 1992).

—— *Seductive Forms; Women's Amatory Fiction from 1684 to 1740* (Oxford, 1992).

Brown, Laura, 'The Romance of Empire: *Oroonoko* and the Trade in Slaves', in Laura Brown and Felicity Nussbaum (eds.), *The New Eighteenth Century* (London, 1987).

Ferguson, Margaret W., 'Juggling the Categories of Race, Class, and Gender: Aphra Behn's *Oroonoko*', in Margo Hendricks and Patricia Parker (eds.), *Women, 'Race', and Writing* (London, 1994).

Ferguson, Moira, *Subject to Others: British Women Writers and Colonial Slavery, 1670–1834* (London, 1992).

Fogarty, Anne, 'Violence and Representation in Aphra Behn's *Oroonoko*', in Carl Plasa and Betty J. Ring (eds.), *The Discourse of Slavery* (London, 1994).

Hulme, Peter, *Colonial Encounters: Europe and the Native Caribbean* (London, 1986).

Messenger, Ann, 'Novel into Play: Aphra Behn and Thomas Southerne', in *His and Hers: Essays in Restoration and Eighteenth-Century Literature* (Lexington, Ky., 1986).

Pearson, Jacqueline, 'Gender and Narrative in the Fiction of Aphra Behn', *Review of English Studies*, 42/165 (Feb. 1991), 40–56; 166 (May 1991), 179–90.

Spencer, Jane, *The Rise of the Woman Novelist* (Oxford, 1986).

GENERAL

Castle, Terry, *Masquerade and Civilisation* (Stanford, 1986).

Chambers, Ross, *Story and Situation* (Minneapolis, 1984).

Chernaik, Warren, *Liberty and Love* (Oxford, 1995).

Donoghue, Emma, *Passions Between Women: British Lesbian Culture 1668–1801* (London, 1994).

Foucault, Michel, 'What is an Author?' in Paul Rabinow (ed.), *The Foucault Reader* (Harmondsworth, 1984), 101–20.

Gallagher, Catherine, *Nobody's Story: The Vanishing Acts of Women Writers in the Marketplace, 1670–1820* (Oxford, 1994).

Greer, Germaine, *et al.*, *Kissing the Rod: An Anthology of Seventeenth-Century Women's Verse* (London, 1988).

Hobby, Elaine, *Virtue of Necessity* (London, 1988).

Kamuf, Peggy, *Fictions of Feminine Desire* (Lincoln, 1982).

Jones, Ann Rosalind, and Stallybrass, Peter, 'Fetishizing Gender: Constructing the Hermaphrodite in Renaissance Europe', in Julia

Epstein and Kristina Straub (eds.), *Bodyguards: The Cultural Politics of Gender Ambiguity* (London, 1991).

Sypher, Wylie, *Guinea's Captive Kings* (1942; repr. New York, 1969).

Todd, Janet, *The Sign of Angellica* (London, 1989).

Shevelow, Kathryn, *Women and Print Culture* (London, 1989).

Index

Recent and Forthcoming Titles in the New Series of

WRITERS AND THEIR WORK

―――――――――――

"...this series promises to outshine its own previously high reputation."
Times Higher Education Supplement

"...will build into a fine multi-volume critical encyclopaedia of English literature."
Library Review & Reference Review

"...Excellent, informative, readable, and recommended."
NATE News

"...promises to be a rare series of creative scholarship."
Times Educational Supplement

WRITERS AND THEIR WORK

RECENT & FORTHCOMING TITLES

Title	Author
Aphra Behn	*Sue Wiseman*
Angela Carter	*Lorna Sage*
Children's Literature	*Kimberley Reynolds*
John Clare	*John Lucas*
Joseph Conrad	*Cedric Watts*
John Donne	*Stevie Davies*
Henry Fielding	*Jenny Uglow*
Elizabeth Gaskell	*Kate Flint*
William Golding	*Kevin McCarron*
Hamlet	*Ann Thompson & Neil Taylor*
David Hare	*Jeremy Ridgman*
Tony Harrison	*Joe Kelleher*
William Hazlitt	*J.B. Priestley; R.L. Brett (introduction by Michael Foot)*
George Herbert	*T.S. Eliot (introduction by Peter Porter)*
Henry James - The Later Writing	*Barbara Hardy*
King Lear	*Terence Hawkes*
Doris Lessing	*Elizabeth Maslen*
David Lodge	*Bernard Bergonzi*
Christopher Marlowe	*Thomas Healy*
Andrew Marvell	*Annabel Patterson*
Ian McEwan	*Kiernan Ryan*
Walter Pater	*Laurel Brake*
Jean Rhys	*Helen Carr*
Dorothy Richardson	*Carol Watts*
The Sensation Novel	*Lyn Pykett*
Edmund Spenser	*Colin Burrow*
Leo Tolstoy	*John Bayley*
Charlotte Yonge	*Alethea Hayter*

TITLES IN PREPARATION

Title	Author
Peter Ackroyd	*Susana Onega*
Antony and Cleopatra	*Ken Parker*
W.H. Auden	*Stan Smith*
Jane Austen	*Robert Clark*
Elizabeth Bowen	*Maud Ellmann*
Emily Brontë	*Stevie Davies*
A.S. Byatt	*Richard Todd*
Lord Byron	*J. Drummond Bone*
Geoffrey Chaucer	*Steve Ellis*
Caryl Churchill	*Elaine Aston*
S.T. Coleridge	*Stephen Bygrave*
Charles Dickens	*Rod Mengham*

TITLES IN PREPARATION

Title	Author
George Eliot	*Josephine McDonagh*
E.M. Forster	*Nicholas Royle*
Brian Friel	*Geraldine Higgins*
Graham Greene	*Peter Mudford*
Thomas Hardy	*Peter Widdowson*
Seamus Heaney	*Andrew Murphy*
Henry IV	*Peter Bogdanov*
Henrik Ibsen	*Sally Ledger*
James Joyce	*Steven Connor*
Rudyard Kipling	*Jan Montefiore*
Franz Kafka	*Michael Wood*
John Keats	*Kelvin Everest*
Philip Larkin	*Laurence Lerner*
D.H. Lawrence	*Linda Ruth Williams*
A Midsummer Night's Dream	*Helen Hackett*
William Morris	*Anne Janowitz*
Brian Patten	*Linda Cookson*
Alexander Pope	*Pat Rogers*
Sylvia Plath	*Elizabeth Bronfen*
Richard II	*Margaret Healy*
Lord Rochester	*Peter Porter*
Romeo and Juliet	*Sasha Roberts*
Christina Rossetti	*Kathryn Burlinson*
Salman Rushdie	*Damian Grant*
Stevie Smith	*Alison Light*
Sir Walter Scott	*John Sutherland*
Wole Soyinka	*Mpalive Msiska*
Jonathan Swift	*Claude Rawson*
The Tempest	*Gordon McMullan*
J.R.R. Tolkien	*Charles Moseley*
Mary Wollstonecraft	*Jane Moore*
Evelyn Waugh	*Malcolm Bradbury*
Angus Wilson	*Peter Conradi*
Virginia Woolf	*Laura Marcus*
William Wordsworth	*Nicholas Roe*
Working Class Fiction	*Ian Haywood*
W.B. Yeats	*Ed Larrissy*